OLD MOORE'S

HOROSCOPE
AND ASTRAL
DIARY

AQUARIUS

OLD MOORE'S

HOROSCOPE AND ASTRAL DIARY

AQUARIUS

foulsham

LONDON • NEW YORK • TORONTO • SYDNEY

foulsham

The Oriel, Thames Valley Court, 183–187 Bath Road, Slough,
Berkshire SL1 4AA, England

Foulsham books can be found in all good bookshops or direct from
www.foulsham.com

ISBN: 978-0-572-03502-0

Copyright © 2009 W. Foulsham & Co. Ltd.

A CIP record for this book is available from the British Library

Printed in Great Britain by CPI Cox & Wyman, Reading, RG1 8EX

CONTENTS

INTRODUCTION

Welcome to *Old Moore's Astral Diary* for the year 2010. The tradition of Old Moore and his astrological prowess goes right back to the 17th century and during that whole period Old Moore has been keeping track of Sun, Moon and planetary movement in order to provide humanity with the best knowledge of day-to-day astrology available.

These days humanity is slightly less fatalistic about the part the stars and planets play in our lives than it once was. Rather than seeing the zodiac as a harbinger of a good or bad fate, modern astrologers deal with the subtle interplay taking place above our heads. Astrology offers a better insight into the 'trends' that surround our lives at any particular time. When we are able to recognise how this or that solar, lunar or planetary position is likely to shape our days we can avoid certain actions or simply act at the right time to take advantage of what is on offer.

With the Astral Diary you can learn the best times to take advantage of positive monetary trends, choose when to pursue relationships and decide whether the time is right to make changes. Will you approach a day positively or with a little trepidation? This is the sort of question Old Moore can answer, and the Astral Diary gives you the chance to maximise your potential. When you see the sign ☿, this means that the planet Mercury is 'retrograde' at that time. Retrograde means that it appears to be moving backwards in space when viewed from Earth, and it indicates a little human disruption as a result. Mercury rules communication so you might expect a few setbacks in this area during this time. The Astral Diary also has space for you to add your own notes and comments.

Old Moore's Astral Diary is much more than a mere astrology book. It lets you look much deeper into your own individual nature. All that you are as an individual is reflected not only in the day but also in the time of day you were born. Your nature also responds to the position of heavenly bodies such as the Moon and the planet Venus. Using the unique tables in the Astral Diary you can work out exactly why you are the sort of person you turned out to be. Once in possession of this information you can deal much more effectively with the twists and turns of life and you will know better how to react to all trends.

Everything within your unique makeup is reflected within your astrological profile. Using the Astral Diary you can get close to the essence of planetary interplay, which in a moment-by-moment sense helps to shape your personality. Astrology can help you to maximise your potential and take those actions that lead to a happier life. Consulting *Old Moore's Astral Diary* will make you more aware of yourself, and is a fascinating way to register the very heartbeat of the solar system of which we are all a part.

Old Moore extends his customary greeting to all people of the Earth and offers his age-old wishes for a happy and prosperous period ahead.

THE ESSENCE OF AQUARIUS

Exploring the Personality of Aquarius the Water Carrier

(21ST JANUARY–19TH FEBRUARY)

What's in a sign?

Oh, what a wonderful person you can be! Despite a number of contradictions and one of the most complicated natures to be found anywhere in the zodiac, you certainly know how to make friends and influence people. Your ruling planet is Uranus, one of the more recently discovered members of the solar system's family. It rules modern communications, such as radio and television, and also has a response to the recent discoveries of science. It is within the world of 'the modern' that you reside and you have little or no difficulty keeping up with the ever-increasing pace of life.

People naturally like you and it's not surprising. You are open, liberal, and rarely judgemental, and you are often surrounded by deeply original and even eccentric types. Life to you is a storybook full of fascinating tales. Aquarians amass information 'on the hoof' and very little passes you by. Understanding what makes others tick is meat and drink to you and proves to be a source of endless joy. Unlike the other Air signs of Gemini and Libra, you are able to spend long hours on your own if necessary and always keep your mind active.

Aquarians have great creative potential; they are refined, often extremely well educated and they remain totally classless. This makes it easy for you to get on with just about any sort of person and also explains your general success in the material world. You are fascinating, original, thought-provoking and even quite deep on occasions. Matters that take months for others to synthesise, you can absorb in minutes. It is clear to everyone that you are one of life's natural leaders, but when you head any organisation you do so by co-operation and example because you are not in the least authoritarian.

In love you can be ardent and sincere – for a while at least. You need to be loved and it's true that deeply personal relationships can be a problem to you if they are not supplying what is most important to you. Few people know the real you, because your nature exists on so many different levels. For this reason alone you defy analysis and tend to remain outside the scope of orthodoxy. And because people can't weigh you up adequately, you appear to be more fascinating than ever.

Aquarius resources

Your chief resource has to be originality. Like a precious Fabergé Egg you are a single creation, unique and quite unlike anything else to be found anywhere in the world. Of course, used wrongly, this can make you seem odd or even downright peculiar. But Aquarians usually have a knack for creating the best possible impression. The chances are that you dress in your own way and speak the words that occur to you, and that you have a side to your nature that shuns convention. Despite this you know how to adapt when necessary. As a result your dinner parties would sport guests of a wide variety of types and stations. All of these people think they know the 'real you' and remain committed to helping you as much as they can.

The natural adaptability that goes along with being an Aquarian makes it possible for you to turn your hand to many different projects. And because you are from an Air sign, you can undertake a variety of tasks at the same time. This makes for a busy life, but being on the go is vital for you and you only tire when you are forced into jobs that you find demeaning, pointless or downright dull.

All of the above combines to make a nature that has 'resourcefulness' as its middle name. Arriving at a given set of circumstances – say a specific task that has to be undertaken – you first analyse what is required. Having done so you get cracking and invariably manage to impress all manner of people with your dexterity, attention to detail and downright intelligence. You can turn work into a social event, or derive financial gain from your social life. Activity is the keyword and you don't really differentiate between the various components of life as many people would.

Success depends on a number of different factors. You need to be doing things you enjoy as much as you can and you simply cannot be held back or bound to follow rules that appear to make no sense to you. You respond well to kindness, and generally receive it because you are so considerate yourself. But perhaps your greatest skill of all is your ability to make a silk purse out of a sow's ear. You are never stuck for an idea and rarely let financial restrictions get in your way.

Beneath the surface

'What you see is what you get' could never really be considered a sensible or accurate statement when applied to the sign of Aquarius. It's difficult enough for you to know the way your complicated mind works, and almost impossible for others to sort out the tangle of possibilities. Your mind can be as untidy as a tatty workbox on occasions and yet at other times you can see through situations with a clarity that would dazzle almost any observer. It really depends on a whole host of circumstances, some of which are inevitably beyond your own control. You are at your best when you are allowed to take charge from the very start of any project, because then your originality of thought comes into play. Your sort of logic is unique to you, so don't expect anyone else to go down the same mental routes that you find easy to follow.

Aquarians are naturally kind and don't tend to discriminate. This is not a considered matter, it's simply the way you are. As a result it is very hard for you to understand prejudice, or individuals who show any form of intolerance. The fairness that you exemplify isn't something that you have to work at – it comes as naturally to you as breathing does.

You can be very peculiar and even a little cranky on occasions. These aspects of your nature are unlikely to have any bearing on your overall popularity, but they do betray a rather unusual mindset that isn't like that of any other zodiac sign. When you feel stressed you tend to withdraw into yourself, which is not really good for you. A much better strategy would be to verbalise what you are thinking, even though this is not always particularly easy to do.

There are many people in the world who think they know you well, but each and every one of them knows only one Aquarian. There are always more, each a unique individual and probably as much of a mystery to you as they would be to all your relatives and friends, that is if any of them suspected just how deep and mysterious you can be. Despite these facts, your mind is clear and concise, enabling you to get to the truth of any given situation almost immediately. You should never doubt your intuitive foresight and, in the main, must always back your hunches. It is rare indeed for you to be totally wrong about the outcome of any potential situation and your genuine originality of thought is the greatest gift providence has bestowed on you.

Making the best of yourself

Interacting with the world is most important to you. Although you can sometimes be a good deal quieter than the other Air signs of Gemini and Libra, you are still a born communicator, with a great need to live your life to the full. If you feel hemmed in or constrained by circumstances, you are not going to show your best face to family, friends or colleagues. That's why you must move heaven and earth to make certain that you are not tied down in any way. Maintaining a sense of freedom is really just a mental state to Aquarius but it is absolutely vital to your well-being.

As far as work is concerned you need to be doing something that allows you the room you need to move. Any occupation that means thinking on your feet would probably suit you fine. All the same you feel more comfortable in administrative surroundings, rather than getting your hands dirty. Any profession that brings change and variety on a daily basis would be best. You are a good team operator, and yet can easily lead from the front. Don't be frightened to show colleagues that you have an original way of looking at life and that you are an inveterate problem solver.

In terms of friendship you tend to be quite catholic in your choice of pals. Making the best of yourself means keeping things that way. You are not naturally jealous yourself but you do tend to attract friends who are. Make it plain that you can't tie yourself down to any one association, no matter how old or close it may be. At least if you do this nobody can suggest that they weren't warned when you wander off to talk to someone else. Personal relationships are a different matter, though it's hardly likely that you would live in the pocket of your partner. In any situation you need space to breathe, and this includes romantic attachments. People who know you well will not try to hem you in.

Don't be frightened to show your unconventional, even wild side to the world at large. You are a bold character, with a great deal to say and a natural warmth that could melt an iceberg. This is the way providence made you and it is only right to use your gifts to the full.

The impressions you give

You are not a naturally secretive person and don't hold back very much when it comes to speaking your mind. It might be suggested therefore that the external and internal Aquarian is more or less the same person. Although generally true, it has to be remembered that you have a multi-faceted nature and one that adapts quickly to changing circumstances. It is this very adaptability that sets you apart in the eyes of the world.

You often make decisions based on intuitive foresight and although many Aquarians are of above average intelligence, you won't always make use of a deep knowledge of any given situation. In essence you often do what seems right, though you tend to act whilst others are still standing around and thinking. This makes you good to have around in a crisis and convinces many of those looking on that you are incredibly capable, relaxed and confident. Of course this isn't always the case, but even a nervous interior tends to breed outward action in the case of your zodiac sign, so the world can be forgiven for jumping to the wrong conclusion.

People like you – there's no doubt about that. However, you must realise that you have a very upfront attitude, which on occasions is going to get you into trouble. Your occasional weirdness, rather than being a turn-off, is likely to stimulate the interest that the world has in you. Those with whom you come into contact invariably find your personality to be attractive, generous, high-spirited and refreshing. For all these reasons it is very unlikely that you would actually make many enemies, even if some folk are clearly jealous of the easy way you have with the world.

One of the great things about Aquarians is that they love to join in. As a result you may find yourself doing all sorts of things that others would find either difficult or frightening. You can be zany, wild and even mad on occasions, but these tendencies will only get you liked all the more. The world will only tire of you if you allow yourself to get down in the dumps or grumpy – a very rare state for Aquarius.

The way forward

In terms of living your life to the full it is probable that you don't need any real advice from an astrologer. Your confidence allows you to go places that would make some people shiver, whilst your intuitive foresight gives you the armoury you need to deal with a world that can sometimes seem threatening. Yet for all this you are not immune to mental turmoil on occasions, and probably spend rather too much time in the fast lane. It's good to rest, a fact that you need to remember the next time you find yourself surrounded by twenty-seven jobs, all of which you are trying to undertake at the same time.

The more the world turns in the direction of information technology, the happier you are likely to become. If others have difficulty in this age of computers, it's likely that you relish the challenges and the opportunities that these artificial intelligences offer. You are happy with New Age concepts and tend to look at the world with compassion and understanding. Despite the fact that you are always on the go, it's rare for you to be moving forward so fast that you forget either the planet that brought you to birth, or the many underprivileged people who inhabit parts of it. You have a highly developed conscience and tend to work for the good of humanity whenever you can.

You might not be constructed of the highest moral fibre known to humanity, a fact that sometimes shows when it comes to romantic attachments. Many Aquarians play the field at some time in their lives and it's certain that you need a personal relationship that keeps you mentally stimulated. Although your exterior can sometimes seem superficial, you have a deep and sensitive soul – so perhaps you should marry a poet, or at least someone who can cope with the twists and turns of the Aquarian mind. Aquarians who tie themselves down too early, or to the wrong sort of individual, invariably end up regretting the fact.

You can be deeply creative and need to live in clean and cheerful surroundings. Though not exactly a minimalist you don't like clutter and constantly need to spring-clean your home – and your mind. Living with others isn't difficult for you, in fact it's essential. Since you are so adaptable you fit in easily to almost any environment, though you will always ultimately stamp your own character onto it. You love to be loved and offer a great deal in return, even if you are occasionally absent when people need you the most. In essence you are in love with life and so perhaps you should not be too surprised to discover that it is very fond of you too.

AQUARIUS ON THE CUSP

Old Moore is often asked how astrological profiles are altered for those people born at either the beginning or the end of a zodiac sign, or, more properly, on the cusps of a sign. In the case of Aquarius this would be on the 21st of January and for two or three days after, and similarly at the end of the sign, probably from the 17th to the 19th of February. In this year's Astral Diaries, once again, Old Moore sets out to explain the differences regarding cuspid signs.

The Capricorn Cusp – January 21st to 23rd

What really sets you apart is a genuinely practical streak that isn't always present in the sign of Aquarius when taken alone. You are likely to have all the joy of life and much of the devil-may-care attitude of your Sun sign, but at the same time you are capable of getting things done in a very positive way. This makes you likely to achieve a higher degree of material success and means that you ally managerial skills with the potential for rolling up your sleeves and taking part in the 'real work' yourself. Alongside this you are able to harness the naturally intuitive qualities of Aquarius in a very matter-of-fact way. Few people would have the ability to pull the wool over your eyes and you are rarely stuck for a solution, even to apparently difficult problems.

You express yourself less well than Aquarius taken alone, and you may have a sort of reserve that leads others to believe that your mind is full of still waters which run very deep. The air of mystery can actually be quite useful, because it masks an ability to react and move quickly when necessary, which is a great surprise to the people around you. However, there are two sides to every coin and if there is a slightly negative quality to this cuspid position it might lie in the fact that you are not quite the communicator that tends to be the case with Aquarius, and you could go through some fairly quiet and introspective phases that those around you would find somewhat difficult to understand. In a positive sense this offers a fairly wistful aspect to your nature that may, in romantic applications, appear very attractive. There is something deeply magnetic about your nature and it isn't quite possible for everyone to understand what makes you tick. Actually this is part of your appeal because there is nothing like curiosity on the part of others to enhance your profile.

Getting things done is what matters the most to you, harnessed to the ability to see the wider picture in life. It's true that not everyone understands your complex nature, but in friendship you are scarcely short of supportive types. Family members can be especially important to you and personal attachments are invariably made for life.

The Pisces Cusp – February 17th to 19th

It appears that you are more of a thinker than most and achieve depths of contemplation that would be totally alien to some signs of the zodiac. Much of your life is given over to the service you show for humanity as a whole but you don't sink into the depths of despair in the way that some Piscean individuals are inclined to do. You are immensely likeable and rarely stuck for a good idea. You know how to enjoy yourself, even if this quality is usually tied to the support and assistance that you constantly give to those around you.

Many of you will already have chosen a profession that somehow fulfils your need to be of service, and it isn't unusual for Pisces-cusp Aquarians to alter their path in life totally if it isn't fulfilling this most basic requirement. When necessary, you can turn your hand to almost anything, generally giving yourself totally to the task in hand, sometimes to the exclusion of everything else. People with this combination often have two very different sorts of career, sometimes managing to do both at the same time. Confidence in practical matters isn't usually lacking, even if you sometimes think that your thought processes are a little bit muddled.

In love you are ardent and more sincere than Aquarius sometimes seems to be. There can be a tinge of jealousy at work now and again in deep relationships, but you are less likely than Pisces to let this show. You tend to be very protective of the people who are most important in your life and these are probably fewer in number than often seems to be the case for Aquarius. Your love of humanity and the needs it has of you are of supreme importance and you barely let a day pass without offering some sort of assistance. For this reason, and many others, you are a much loved individual and show your most caring face to the world for the majority of your life. Material success can be hard to come by at first, but it isn't really an aspect of life that worries you too much in any case. It is far more important for you to be content with your lot and, if you are happy, it seems that more or less everything else tends to follow.

AQUARIUS AND ITS ASCENDANTS

The nature of every individual on the planet is composed of the rich variety of zodiac signs and planetary positions that were present at the time of their birth. Your Sun sign, which in your case is Aquarius, is one of the many factors when it comes to assessing the unique person you are. Probably the most important consideration, other than your Sun sign, is to establish the zodiac sign that was rising over the eastern horizon at the time that you were born. This is your Ascending or Rising sign. Most popular astrology fails to take account of the Ascendant, and yet its importance remains with you from the very moment of your birth, through every day of your life. The Ascendant is evident in the way you approach the world, and so, when meeting a person for the first time, it is this astrological influence that you are most likely to notice first. Our Ascending sign essentially represents what we appear to be, while the Sun sign is what we feel inside ourselves.

The Ascendant also has the potential for modifying our overall nature. For example, if you were born at a time of day when Aquarius was passing over the eastern horizon (this would be around the time of dawn) then you would be classed as a double Aquarian. As such, you would typify this zodiac sign, both internally and in your dealings with others. However, if your Ascendant sign turned out to be a Fire sign, such as Aries, there would be a profound alteration of nature, away from the expected qualities of Aquarius.

One of the reasons why popular astrology often ignores the Ascendant is that it has always been rather difficult to establish. Old Moore has found a way to make this possible by devising an easy-to-use table, which you will find on page 158 of this book. Using this, you can establish your Ascendant sign at a glance. You will need to know your rough time of birth, then it is simply a case of following the instructions.

For those readers who have no idea of their time of birth it might be worth allowing a good friend, or perhaps your partner, to read through the section that follows this introduction. Someone who deals with you on a regular basis may easily discover your Ascending sign, even though you could have some difficulty establishing it for yourself. A good understanding of this component of your nature is essential if you want to be aware of that 'other person' who is responsible for the way you make contact with the world at large. Your Sun sign, Ascendant sign, and the other pointers in this book will, together, allow you a far better understanding of what makes you tick as an individual. Peeling back the different layers of your astrological make-up can be an enlightening experience, and the Ascendant may represent one of the most important layers of all.

Aquarius with Aquarius Ascendant

You are totally unique and quite original, so much so that very few people could claim to understand what makes you tick. Routines get on your nerves and you need to be out there doing something most of the time. Getting where you want to go in life isn't too difficult, except that when you arrive, your destination might not look half so interesting as it did before. You are well liked and should have many friends. This is not to say that your pals have much in common with each other, because you choose from a wide cross-section of people. Although folks see you as being very reasonable in the main, you are capable of being quite cranky on occasions. Your intuition is extremely strong and is far less likely to let you down than would be the case with some individuals.

Travel is very important to you and you will probably live for some time in a different part of your own country, or even in another part of the world. At work you are more than capable, but do need something to do that you find personally stimulating, because you are not very good at constant routine. You can be relied upon to use your originality and find solutions that are instinctive and brilliant. Most people are very fond of you.

Aquarius with Pisces Ascendant

Here we find the originality of Aquarius balanced by the very sensitive qualities of Pisces, and it makes for a very interesting combination. When it comes to understanding other people you are second to none, but it's certain that you are more instinctive than either Pisces or Aquarius when taken alone. You are better at routines than Aquarius, but also relish a challenge more than the typical Piscean would. Active and enterprising, you tend to know what you want from life, but consideration of others, and the world at large, will always be part of the scenario. People with this combination often work on behalf of humanity and are to be found in social work, the medical profession and religious institutions. As far as beliefs are concerned you don't conform to established patterns, and yet may get closer to the truth of the Creator than many deep theological thinkers have ever been able to do. Acting on impulse as much as you do means that not everyone understands the way your mind works, but your popularity will invariably see you through.

Passionate and deeply sensitive, you are able to negotiate the twists and turns of a romantic life that is hardly likely to be run-of-the-mill. In the end, however, you should be able to discover a very deep personal and spiritual happiness.

Aquarius with Aries Ascendant

If ever anyone could be accused of setting off immediately, but slowly, it has to be you. These are very contradictory signs and the differences will express themselves in a variety of ways. One thing is certain, you have tremendous tenacity and will see a job through patiently from beginning to end, without tiring on the way and ensuring that every detail is taken care of properly. This combination often brings good health and a great capacity for continuity, particularly in terms of the length of life. You are certainly not as argumentative as the typical Aries, but you do know how to get your own way, which is just as well because you are usually thinking on behalf of everyone else and not just on your own account.

At home you can relax, which is a blessing for Aries, though in fact you seldom choose to do so because you always have some project or other on the go. You probably enjoy knocking down and rebuilding walls, though this is a practical tendency and not responsive to relationships, in which you are ardent and sincere. Impetuosity is as close to your heart as is the case for any type of subject, though you certainly have the ability to appear patient and steady. But it's just a front, isn't it?

Aquarius with Taurus Ascendant

There is nothing that you fail to think about deeply and with great intensity. You are wise, honest and very scientific in your approach to life. Routines are necessary in life but you have most of them sorted out well in advance and so always have time to look at the next interesting fact. If you don't spend all your time watching documentaries on the television set, you make a good friend and love to socialise. Most of the great discoveries of the world were probably made by people with this sort of astrological combination, though your nature is rather 'odd' on occasions and so can be rather difficult for others to understand.

You may be most surprised when others tell you that you are eccentric, but you don't really mind too much because for half of the time you are not inhabiting the same world as the rest of us. Because you can be delightfully dotty you are probably much loved and cherished by your friends, of which there are likely to be many. Family members probably adore you too, and you can be guaranteed to entertain anyone with whom you come into contact. The only fly in the ointment is that you sometimes lose track of reality, whatever that might be, and fly high in your own atmosphere of rarefied possibilities.

Aquarius with Gemini Ascendant

If you were around in the 1960s there is every chance that you were the first to go around with flowers in your hair. You are unconventional, original, quirky and entertaining. Few people would fail to notice your presence and you take life as it comes, even though on most occasions you are firmly in the driving seat. It all probability you care very much about the planet on which you live and the people with whom you share it. Not everyone understands you, but that does not really matter, for you have more than enough communication skills to put your message across intact. You should avoid wearing yourself out by worrying about things that you cannot control, and you definitely gain from taking time out to meditate. However, whether or not you allow yourself that luxury remains to be seen.

If you are not the most communicative form of Gemini subject then you must come a close second. Despite this fact much of what you have to say makes real sense and you revel in the company of interesting, intelligent and stimulating people, whose opinions on a host of matters will add to your own considerations. You are a true original in every sense of the word and the mere fact of your presence in the world is bound to add to the enjoyment of life experienced by the many people with whom you make contact.

Aquarius with Cancer Ascendant

The truly original spark, for which the sign of Aquarius is famed, can only enhance the caring qualities of Cancer, and is also inclined to bring the Crab out of its shell to a much greater extent than would be the case with certain other zodiac combinations. Aquarius is a party animal and never arrives without something interesting to say, which is doubly the case when the reservoir of emotion and consideration that is Cancer is feeding the tap. Your nature can be rather confusing for even you to deal with, but you are inspirational, bright, charming and definitely fun to be around.

The Cancer element in your nature means that you care about your home and the people to whom you are related. You are also a good and loyal friend, who would keep attachments for much longer than could be expected for Aquarius alone. You love to travel and can be expected to make many journeys to far-off places during your life. Some attention will have to be paid to your health, because you are capable of burning up masses of nervous energy, often without getting the periods of rest and contemplation that are essential to the deeper qualities of the sign of Cancer. Nevertheless you have determination, resilience and a refreshing attitude that lifts the spirits of the people in your vicinity.

Aquarius with Leo Ascendant

All associations with Aquarius bring originality, and you are no exception. You aspire to do your best most of the time but manage to achieve your objectives in an infinitely amusing and entertaining way. Not that you set out to do so, because if you are an actor on the stage of life, it seems as though you are a natural one. There is nothing remotely pretentious about your breezy personality or your ability to occupy the centre of any stage. This analogy is quite appropriate because you probably like the theatre. Being in any situation when reality is suspended for a while suits you down to the ground, and in any case you may regularly ask yourself if you even recognise what reality is. Always asking questions, both of yourself and the world at large, you soldier on relentlessly, though not to the exclusion of having a good time on the way.

Keeping to tried and tested paths is not your way. You are a natural trailblazer who is full of good ideas and who has the energy to put them into practice. You care deeply for the people who play an important part in your life but are wise enough to allow them the space they need to develop their own personalities along the way. Most people like you, many love you, and one or two think that you really are the best thing since sliced bread.

Aquarius with Virgo Ascendant

How could anyone make the convention unconventional? Well, if anyone can manage, you can. There are great contradictions here, because on the one hand you always want to do the expected thing, but the Aquarian quality within your nature loves to surprise everyone on the way. If you don't always know what you are thinking or doing, it's a pretty safe bet that others won't either, so it's important on occasions really to stop and think. However this is not a pressing concern, because you tend to live a fairly happy life and muddle through no matter what. Other people tend to take to you well and it is likely that you will have many friends. You tend to be bright and cheerful and can approach even difficult tasks with the certainty that you have the skills necessary to see them through to their conclusion. Give and take are important factors in the life of any individual and particularly so in your case. Because you can stretch yourself in order to understand what makes other people think and act in the way that they do, you have the reputation of being a good friend and a reliable colleague.

In love you can be somewhat more fickle than the typical Virgoan, and yet you are always interesting to live with. Where you are, things happen, and you mix a sparkling wit with deep insights.

Aquarius with Libra Ascendant

Stand by for a truly interesting and very inspiring combination here, but one that is sometimes rather difficult to fathom, even for the sort of people who believe themselves to be very perceptive. The reason for this could be that any situation has to be essentially fixed and constant in order to get a handle on it, and this is certainly not the case for the Aquarian–Libran type. The fact is that both these signs are Air signs, and to a certain extent as unpredictable as the wind itself.

To most people you seem to be original, frank, free and very outspoken. Not everything you do makes sense to others and if you were alive during the hippy era, it is likely that you went around with flowers in your hair, for you are a free-thinking idealist at heart. With age you mature somewhat, but never too much, because you will always see the strange, the comical and the original in life. This is what keeps you young and is one of the factors that makes you so very attractive to members of the opposite sex. Many people will want to 'adopt' you and you are at your very best when in company.

Much of your effort is expounded on others and yet, unless you discipline yourself a good deal, personal relationships of the romantic sort can bring certain difficulties. Careful planning is necessary.

Aquarius with Scorpio Ascendant

Here we have a combination that shows much promise and a flexibility that allows many changes in direction, allied to a power to succeed, sometimes very much against all the odds. Aquarius lightens the load of the Scorpio mind, turning the depths into potential, and intuitive foresight into a means for getting on in life. There are depths here, because even airy Aquarius isn't so easy to understand, and it is therefore a fact that some people with this combination will always be something of a mystery. However, even this fact can be turned to your advantage because it means that people will always be looking at you. Confidence is so often the key to success in life and the Scorpio–Aquarius mix offers this, or at least appears to do so. Even when this is not entirely the case, the fact that everyone around you believes it to be true is often enough.

You are usually good to know, and show a keen intellect and a deep intelligence, aided by a fascination for life that knows no bounds. When at your best you are giving, understanding, balanced and active. On those occasions when things are not going well for you, beware of a stubborn streak and the need to be sensational. Keep it light and happy and you won't go far wrong. Most of you are very, very much loved.

19

Aquarius with Sagittarius Ascendant

There is an original streak to your nature which is very attractive to the people with whom you share your life. Always different, ever on the go and anxious to try out the next experiment in life, you are interested in almost everything, and yet deeply attached to almost nothing. Everyone you know thinks that you are a little 'odd', but you probably don't mind them believing this because you know it to be true. In fact it is possible that you positively relish your eccentricity, which sets you apart from the common herd and means that you are always going to be noticed.

Although it may seem strange with this combination of Air and Fire, you can be distinctly cool on occasions, have a deep and abiding love of your own company now and again and won't be easily understood. Love comes fairly easily to you but there are times when you are accused of being self-possessed, self-indulgent and not willing enough to fall in line with the wishes of those around you. Despite this you walk on and on down your own path. At heart you are an extrovert and you love to party, often late into the night. Luxury appeals to you, though it tends to be of the transient sort. Travel could easily play a major and a very important part in your life.

Aquarius with Capricorn Ascendant

Here the determination of Capricorn is assisted by a slightly more adaptable quality and an off-beat personality that tends to keep everyone else guessing. You don't care to be quite so predictable as the archetypal Capricorn would be, and there is a more idealistic quality here, or at least one that shows more. A greater number of friends than Capricorn usually keeps is likely, though less than the true Aquarian would gather. Few people doubt your sincerity, though by no means all of them understand what makes you tick. Unfortunately you are not in a position to help them out, because you are not too sure yourself. All the same, you muddle through and can be very capable when the mood takes you.

Being a natural traveller, you love to see new places and would be quite fascinated by cultures that are very different to your own. People with this combination are inclined to spend some time living abroad and may even settle there. You look out for the underdog and will always have time for a good cause, no matter what it takes to help. In romantic terms you are a reliable partner, though with a slightly wayward edge which, if anything, tends to make you even more attractive. Listen to your intuition, which is well honed and rarely lets you down. Generally speaking you are very popular.

THE MOON AND THE PART IT PLAYS IN YOUR LIFE

In astrology the Moon is probably the single most important heavenly body after the Sun. Its unique position, as partner to the Earth on its journey around the solar system, means that the Moon appears to pass through the signs of the zodiac extremely quickly. The zodiac position of the Moon at the time of your birth plays a great part in personal character and is especially significant in the build-up of your emotional nature.

Sun Moon Cycles

The first lunar cycle deals with the part the position of the Moon plays relative to your Sun sign. I have made the fluctuations of this pattern easy for you to understand by means of a simple cyclic graph. It appears on the first page of each 'Your Month At A Glance', under the title 'Highs and Lows'. The graph displays the lunar cycle and you will soon learn to understand how its movements have a bearing on your level of energy and your abilities.

Your Own Moon Sign

Discovering the position of the Moon at the time of your birth has always been notoriously difficult because tracking the complex zodiac positions of the Moon is not easy. This process has been reduced to three simple stages with Old Moore's unique Lunar Tables. A breakdown of the Moon's zodiac positions can be found from page 25 onwards, so that once you know what your Moon Sign is, you can see what part this plays in the overall build-up of your personal character.

If you follow the instructions on the next page you will soon be able to work out exactly what zodiac sign the Moon occupied on the day that you were born and you can then go on to compare the reading for this position with those of your Sun sign and your Ascendant. It is partly the comparison between these three important positions that goes towards making you the unique individual you are.

HOW TO DISCOVER YOUR MOON SIGN

This is a three-stage process. You may need a pen and a piece of paper but if you follow the instructions below the process should only take a minute or so.

STAGE 1 First of all you need to know the Moon Age at the time of your birth. If you look at Moon Table 1, on page 23, you will find all the years between 1912 and 2010 down the left side. Find the year of your birth and then trace across to the right to the month of your birth. Where the two intersect you will find a number. This is the date of the New Moon in the month that you were born. You now need to count forward the number of days between the New Moon and your own birthday. For example, if the New Moon in the month of your birth was shown as being the 6th and you were born on the 20th, your Moon Age Day would be 14. If the New Moon in the month of your birth came after your birthday, you need to count forward from the New Moon in the previous month, which, if you were born in January, means you must look at December in the previous year. You cannot count from December in the year of your birth, as that month is *after* your birth. Whatever the result, jot this number down so that you do not forget it.

STAGE 2 Take a look at Moon Table 2 on page 24. Down the left hand column look for the date of your birth. Now trace across to the month of your birth. Where the two meet you will find a letter. Copy this letter down alongside your Moon Age Day.

STAGE 3 Moon Table 3 on page 24 will supply you with the zodiac sign the Moon occupied on the day of your birth. Look for your Moon Age Day down the left hand column and then for the letter you found in Stage 2. Where the two converge you will find a zodiac sign and this is the sign occupied by the Moon on the day that you were born.

Your Zodiac Moon Sign Explained

You will find a profile of all zodiac Moon Signs on pages 25 to 28, showing in yet another way how astrology helps to make you into the individual that you are. In each daily entry of the Astral Diary you can find the zodiac position of the Moon for every day of the year. This also allows you to discover your lunar birthdays. Since the Moon passes through all the signs of the zodiac in about a month, you can expect something like twelve lunar birthdays each year. At these times you are likely to be emotionally steady and able to make the sort of decisions that have real, lasting value.

MOON TABLE 1

YEAR	DEC	JAN	FEB	YEAR	DEC	JAN	FEB	YEAR	DEC	JAN	FEB
1912	9	18	17	1945	4	14	12	1978	29	9	7
1913	27	7	6	1946	23	3	2	1979	18	27	26
1914	17	25	24	1947	12	21	19	1980	7	16	15
1915	6	15	14	1948	1/30	11	9	1981	26	6	4
1916	25	5	3	1949	19	29	27	1982	15	25	23
1917	13	24	22	1950	9	18	16	1983	4	14	13
1918	2	12	11	1951	28	7	6	1984	22	3	1
1919	21	1/31	–	1952	17	26	25	1985	12	21	19
1920	10	20	19	1953	6	15	14	1986	1/30	10	9
1921	29	9	8	1954	25	5	3	1987	20	29	28
1922	18	27	26	1955	14	24	22	1988	9	19	17
1923	8	17	15	1956	2	13	11	1989	28	7	6
1924	26	6	5	1957	21	1/30	–	1990	17	26	25
1925	15	24	23	1958	10	19	18	1991	6	15	14
1926	5	14	12	1959	29	9	7	1992	24	4	3
1927	24	3	2	1960	18	27	26	1993	14	23	22
1928	12	21	19	1961	7	16	15	1994	2	11	10
1929	1/30	11	9	1962	26	6	5	1995	22	1/30	–
1930	19	29	28	1963	15	25	23	1996	10	20	18
1931	9	18	17	1964	4	14	13	1997	28	9	7
1932	27	7	6	1965	22	3	1	1998	18	27	26
1933	17	25	24	1966	12	21	19	1999	7	17	16
1934	6	15	14	1967	1/30	10	9	2000	26	6	4
1935	25	5	3	1968	20	29	28	2001	15	25	23
1936	13	24	22	1969	9	19	17	2002	4	13	12
1937	2	12	11	1970	28	7	6	2003	23	3	1
1938	21	1/31	–	1971	17	26	25	2004	11	21	20
1939	10	20	19	1972	6	15	14	2005	30	10	9
1940	28	9	8	1973	25	5	4	2006	20	29	28
1941	18	27	26	1974	14	24	22	2007	9	18	16
1942	8	16	15	1975	3	12	11	2008	27	8	6
1943	27	6	4	1976	21	1/31	29	2009	16	26	25
1944	15	25	24	1977	10	19	18	2010	6	15	14

TABLE 2

DAY	JAN	FEB
1	A	D
2	A	D
3	A	D
4	A	D
5	A	D
6	A	D
7	A	D
8	A	D
9	A	D
10	A	E
11	B	E
12	B	E
13	B	E
14	B	E
15	B	E
16	B	E
17	B	E
18	B	E
19	B	E
20	B	F
21	C	F
22	C	F
23	C	F
24	C	F
25	C	F
26	C	F
27	C	F
28	C	F
29	C	F
30	C	–
31	D	–

MOON TABLE 3

M/D	A	B	C	D	E	F	G
0	CP	AQ	AQ	AQ	PI	PI	PI
1	AQ	AQ	AQ	PI	PI	PI	AR
2	AQ	AQ	PI	PI	PI	AR	AR
3	AQ	PI	PI	PI	AR	AR	AR
4	PI	PI	AR	AR	AR	AR	TA
5	PI	AR	AR	AR	TA	TA	TA
6	AR	AR	AR	TA	TA	TA	GE
7	AR	AR	TA	TA	TA	GE	GE
8	AR	TA	TA	TA	GE	GE	GE
9	TA	TA	GE	GE	GE	CA	CA
10	TA	GE	GE	GE	CA	CA	CA
11	GE	GE	GE	CA	CA	CA	LE
12	GE	GE	CA	CA	CA	LE	LE
13	GE	CA	CA	LE	LE	LE	LE
14	CA	CA	LE	LE	LE	VI	VI
15	CA	LE	LE	LE	VI	VI	VI
16	LE	LE	LE	VI	VI	VI	LI
17	LE	LE	VI	VI	VI	LI	LI
18	LE	VI	VI	VI	LI	LI	LI
19	VI	VI	VI	LI	LI	LI	SC
20	VI	LI	LI	LI	SC	SC	SC
21	LI	LI	LI	SC	SC	SC	SA
22	LI	LI	SC	SC	SC	SA	SA
23	LI	SC	SC	SC	SA	SA	SA
24	SC	SC	SC	SA	SA	SA	CP
25	SC	SA	SA	SA	CP	CP	CP
26	SA	SA	SA	CP	CP	CP	AQ
27	SA	SA	CP	CP	AQ	AQ	AQ
28	SA	CP	CP	AQ	AQ	AQ	AQ
29	CP	CP	CP	AQ	AQ	AQ	PI

AR = Aries, TA = Taurus, GE = Gemini, CA = Cancer, LE = Leo, VI = Virgo, LI = Libra, SC = Scorpio, SA = Sagittarius, CP = Capricorn, AQ = Aquarius, PI = Pisces

MOON SIGNS

Moon in Aries

You have a strong imagination, courage, determination and a desire to do things in your own way and forge your own path through life.

Originality is a key attribute; you are seldom stuck for ideas although your mind is changeable and you could take the time to focus on individual tasks. Often quick-tempered, you take orders from few people and live life at a fast pace. Avoid health problems by taking regular time out for rest and relaxation.

Emotionally, it is important that you talk to those you are closest to and work out your true feelings. Once you discover that people are there to help, there is less necessity for you to do everything yourself.

Moon in Taurus

The Moon in Taurus gives you a courteous and friendly manner, which means you are likely to have many friends.

The good things in life mean a lot to you, as Taurus is an Earth sign that delights in experiences which please the senses. Hence you are probably a lover of good food and drink, which may in turn mean you need to keep an eye on the bathroom scales, especially as looking good is also important to you.

Emotionally you are fairly stable and you stick by your own standards. Taureans do not respond well to change. Intuition also plays an important part in your life.

Moon in Gemini

You have a warm-hearted character, sympathetic and eager to help others. At times reserved, you can also be articulate and chatty: this is part of the paradox of Gemini, which always brings duplicity to the nature. You are interested in current affairs, have a good intellect, and are good company and likely to have many friends. Most of your friends have a high opinion of you and would be ready to defend you should the need arise. However, this is usually unnecessary, as you are quite capable of defending yourself in any verbal confrontation.

Travel is important to your inquisitive mind and you find intellectual stimulus in mixing with people from different cultures. You also gain much from reading, writing and the arts but you do need plenty of rest and relaxation in order to avoid fatigue.

Moon in Cancer

The Moon in Cancer at the time of birth is a fortunate position as Cancer is the Moon's natural home. This means that the qualities of compassion and understanding given by the Moon are especially enhanced in your nature, and you are friendly and sociable and cope well with emotional pressures. You cherish home and family life, and happily do the domestic tasks. Your surroundings are important to you and you hate squalor and filth. You are likely to have a love of music and poetry.

Your basic character, although at times changeable like the Moon itself, depends on symmetry. You aim to make your surroundings comfortable and harmonious, for yourself and those close to you.

Moon in Leo

The best qualities of the Moon and Leo come together to make you warm-hearted, fair, ambitious and self-confident. With good organisational abilities, you invariably rise to a position of responsibility in your chosen career. This is fortunate as you don't enjoy being an 'also-ran' and would rather be an important part of a small organisation than a menial in a large one.

You should be lucky in love, and happy, provided you put in the effort to make a comfortable home for yourself and those close to you. It is likely that you will have a love of pleasure, sport, music and literature. Life brings you many rewards, most of them as a direct result of your own efforts, although you may be luckier than average and ready to make the best of any situation.

Moon in Virgo

You are endowed with good mental abilities and a keen receptive memory, but you are never ostentatious or pretentious. Naturally quite reserved, you still have many friends, especially of the opposite sex. Marital relationships must be discussed carefully and worked at so that they remain harmonious, as personal attachments can be a problem if you do not give them your full attention.

Talented and persevering, you possess artistic qualities and are a good homemaker. Earning your honours through genuine merit, you work long and hard towards your objectives but show little pride in your achievements. Many short journeys will be undertaken in your life.

Moon in Libra

With the Moon in Libra you are naturally popular and make friends easily. People like you, probably more than you realise, you bring fun to a party and are a natural diplomat. For all its good points, Libra is not the most stable of astrological signs and, as a result, your emotions can be a little unstable too. Therefore, although the Moon in Libra is said to be good for love and marriage, your Sun sign and Rising sign will have an important effect on your emotional and loving qualities.

You must remember to relate to others in your decision-making. Co-operation is crucial because Libra represents the 'balance' of life that can only be achieved through harmonious relationships. Conformity is not easy for you because Libra, an Air sign, likes its independence.

Moon in Scorpio

Some people might call you pushy. In fact, all you really want to do is to live life to the full and protect yourself and your family from the pressures of life. Take care to avoid giving the impression of being sarcastic or impulsive and use your energies wisely and constructively.

You have great courage and you invariably achieve your goals by force of personality and sheer effort. You are fond of mystery and are good at predicting the outcome of situations and events. Travel experiences can be beneficial to you.

You may experience problems if you do not take time to examine your motives in a relationship, and also if you allow jealousy, always a feature of Scorpio, to cloud your judgement.

Moon in Sagittarius

The Moon in Sagittarius helps to make you a generous individual with humanitarian qualities and a kind heart. Restlessness may be intrinsic as your mind is seldom still. Perhaps because of this, you have a need for change that could lead you to several major moves during your adult life. You are not afraid to stand your ground when you know your judgement is right, you speak directly and have good intuition.

At work you are quick, efficient and versatile and so you make an ideal employee. You need work to be intellectually demanding and do not enjoy tedious routines.

In relationships, you anger quickly if faced with stupidity or deception, though you are just as quick to forgive and forget. Emotionally, there are times when your heart rules your head.

Moon in Capricorn

The Moon in Capricorn makes you popular and likely to come into the public eye in some way. The watery Moon is not entirely comfortable in the Earth sign of Capricorn and this may lead to some difficulties in the early years of life. An initial lack of creative ability and indecision must be overcome before the true qualities of patience and perseverance inherent in Capricorn can show through.

You have good administrative ability and are a capable worker, and if you are careful you can accumulate wealth. But you must be cautious and take professional advice in partnerships, as you are open to deception. You may be interested in social or welfare work, which suit your organisational skills and sympathy for others.

Moon in Aquarius

The Moon in Aquarius makes you an active and agreeable person with a friendly, easy-going nature. Sympathetic to the needs of others, you flourish in a laid-back atmosphere. You are broad-minded, fair and open to suggestion, although sometimes you have an unconventional quality which others can find hard to understand.

You are interested in the strange and curious, and in old articles and places. You enjoy trips to these places and gain much from them. Political, scientific and educational work interests you and you might choose a career in science or technology.

Money-wise, you make gains through innovation and concentration and Lunar Aquarians often tackle more than one job at a time. In love you are kind and honest.

Moon in Pisces

You have a kind, sympathetic nature, somewhat retiring at times, but you always take account of others' feelings and help when you can.

Personal relationships may be problematic, but as life goes on you can learn from your experiences and develop a better understanding of yourself and the world around you.

You have a fondness for travel, appreciate beauty and harmony and hate disorder and strife. You may be fond of literature and would make a good writer or speaker yourself. You have a creative imagination and may come across as an incurable romantic. You have strong intuition, maybe bordering on a mediumistic quality, which sets you apart from the mass. You may not be rich in cash terms, but your personal gifts are worth more than gold.

AQUARIUS IN LOVE

Discover how compatible in love you are with people from the same and other signs of the zodiac. Five stars equals a match made in heaven!

Aquarius meets Aquarius

This is a good match for several reasons. Most importantly, although it sounds arrogant, Aquarians like themselves. At its best, Aquarius is one of the fairest, most caring and genuinely pleasant zodiac signs and so it is only when faced by the difficulties created by others that it shows a less favourable side. Put two Aquarians together and voilà – instant success! Personal and family life should bring more joy. On the whole, a platform for adventure based on solid foundations. Star rating: *****

Aquarius meets Pisces

Zodiac signs that follow each other often have something in common, but this is not the case with Aquarius and Pisces. Both signs are deeply caring, but in different ways. Pisces is one of the deepest zodiac signs, and Aquarius simply isn't prepared to embark on the journey. Pisceans, meanwhile, would probably find Aquarians superficial and even flippant. On the positive side there is potential for a well-balanced relationship, but unless one party is untypical of their zodiac sign, it often doesn't get started. Star rating: **

Aquarius meets Aries

Aquarius is an Air sign, and Air and Fire often work well together, but not in the case of Aries and Aquarius. The average Aquarian lives in what the Ram sees as a fantasy world, so a meeting of minds is unlikely. Of course, the dominant side of Aries could be trained by the devil-may-care attitude of Aquarius. There are meeting points but they are difficult to establish. However, given sufficient time and an open mind on both sides, a degree of happiness is possible. Star rating: **

Aquarius meets Taurus

In any relationship of which Aquarius is a part, surprises abound. It is difficult for Taurus to understand the soul-searching, adventurous, changeable Aquarian, but on the positive side, the Bull is adaptable and can respond well to a dose of excitement. Aquarians are kind and react well to the same quality coming back at them. Both are friendly, capable of deep affection and basically creative. Unfortunately, Taurus simply doesn't know what makes Aquarius tick, which could lead to feelings of isolation, even if these don't always show on the surface. Star rating: **

Aquarius meets Gemini

Aquarius is commonly mistaken for a Water sign, but in fact it's ruled by the Air element, and this is the key to its compatibility with Gemini. Both signs mix freely socially, and each has an insatiable curiosity. There is plenty of action, lots of love, but very little rest, and so great potential for success if they don't wear each other out! Aquarius revels in its own eccentricity, and encourages Gemini to emulate this. Theirs will be an unconventional household, but almost everyone warms to this crazy and unpredictable couple. Star rating: *****

Aquarius meets Cancer

Cancer is often attracted to Aquarius and, as Aquarius is automatically on the side of anyone who fancies it, so there is the potential for something good here. Cancer loves Aquarius' devil-may-care approach to life, but also recognises and seeks to strengthen the basic lack of self-confidence that all Air signs try so hard to keep secret. Both signs are natural travellers and are quite adventurous. Their family life could be unusual, but friends would recognise a caring, sharing household with many different interests shared by people genuinely in love. Star rating: ***

Aquarius meets Leo

The problem here is that Aquarius doesn't think in the general sense of the word, it knows. Leo, on the other hand, is more practical and relies more on logical reasoning, and consequently it doesn't understand Aquarius very well. Aquarians can also appear slightly frosty in their appreciation of others and this, too, will annoy Leo. This is a good match for a business partnership because Aquarius is astute, while Leo is brave, but personally the prognosis is less promising. Tolerance, understanding and forbearance are all needed to make this work. Star rating: **

Aquarius meets Virgo

Aquarius is a strange sign because no matter how well one knows it, it always manages to surprise. For this reason, against the odds, it's quite likely that Aquarius will form a sucessful relationship with Virgo. Aquarius is changeable, unpredictable and often quite odd, while Virgo is steady, a fuss-pot and very practical. Herein lies the key. What one sign needs, the other provides and that may be the surest recipe for success imaginable. On-lookers may not know why the couple are happy, but they will recognise that this is the case. Star rating: ****

Aquarius meets Libra

One of the best combinations imaginable, partly because both are Air signs and so share a common meeting point. But perhaps the more crucial factor is that both signs respect each other. Aquarius loves life and originality, and is quite intellectual. Libra is similar, but more balanced and rather less eccentric. A visit to this couple's house would be entertaining and full of zany wit, activity and excitement. Both are keen to travel and may prefer to 'find themselves' before taking on too many domestic responsibilities. Star rating: *****

Aquarius meets Scorpio

This is a promising and practical combination. Scorpio responds well to Aquarius' persistent exploration of its deep nature and so this generally shy sign becomes lighter, brighter and more inspirational. Meanwhile, Aquarians are rarely as sure of themselves as they like to appear and are reassured by Scorpio's constant, steady and determined support. Both signs want to be kind to each other, which is a good starting point to a relationship that should be warm most of the time and extremely hot occasionally. Star rating: ****

Aquarius meets Sagittarius

Both Sagittarius and Aquarius are into mind games, which may lead to something of an intellectual competition. If one side is happy to be 'bamboozled' it won't be a problem, but it is more likely that the relationship will turn into a competition, which won't auger well for its long-term future. However, on the plus side, both signs are adventurous and sociable, so as long as there is always something new and interesting to do, the match could turn out very well. Star rating: **

Aquarius meets Capricorn

Probably one of the least likely combinations, as Capricorn and Aquarius are unlikely to choose each other in the first place, unless one side is quite untypical of their sign. Capricorn approaches things in a practical way and likes to get things done, while Aquarius works almost exclusively for the moment and relies heavily on intuition. Their attitudes to romance are also diametrically opposed: Aquarius' moods tend to swing from red hot to ice cold in a minute, which is alien to steady Capricorn. Star rating: **

VENUS:
THE PLANET OF LOVE

If you look up at the sky around sunset or sunrise you will often see Venus in close attendance to the Sun. It is arguably one of the most beautiful sights of all and there is little wonder that historically it became associated with the goddess of love. But although Venus does play an important part in the way you view love and in the way others see you romantically, this is only one of the spheres of influence that it enjoys in your overall character.

Venus has a part to play in the more cultured side of your life and has much to do with your appreciation of art, literature, music and general creativity. Even the way you look is responsive to the part of the zodiac that Venus occupied at the start of your life, though this fact is also down to your Sun sign and Ascending sign. If, at the time you were born, Venus occupied one of the more gregarious zodiac signs, you will be more likely to wear your heart on your sleeve, as well as to be more attracted to entertainment, social gatherings and good company. If on the other hand Venus occupied a quiet zodiac sign at the time of your birth, you would tend to be more retiring and less willing to shine in public situations.

It's good to know what part the planet Venus plays in your life for it can have a great bearing on the way you appear to the rest of the world and since we all have to mix with others, you can learn to make the very best of what Venus has to offer you.

One of the great complications in the past has always been trying to establish exactly what zodiac position Venus enjoyed when you were born because the planet is notoriously difficult to track. However, I have solved that problem by creating a table that is exclusive to your Sun sign, which you will find on the following page.

Establishing your Venus sign could not be easier. Just look up the year of your birth on the page opposite and you will see a sign of the zodiac. This was the sign that Venus occupied in the period covered by your sign in that year. If Venus occupied more than one sign during the period, this is indicated by the date on which the sign changed, and the name of the new sign. For instance, if you were born in 1945, Venus was in Pisces until the 12th February, after which time it was in Aries. If you were born before 12th February your Venus sign is Pisces, if you were born on or after 12th February, your Venus sign is Aries. Once you have established the position of Venus at the time of your birth, you can then look in the pages which follow to see how this has a bearing on your life as a whole.

1912 SAGITTARIUS /
  30.1 CAPRICORN
1913 PISCES / 16.2 ARIES
1914 CAPRICORN / 26.1 AQUARIUS /
  19.2 PISCES
1915 SAGITTARIUS / 7.2 CAPRICORN
1916 PISCES / 14.2 ARIES
1917 CAPRICORN / 9.2 AQUARIUS
1918 AQUARIUS
1919 AQUARIUS / 3.2 PISCES
1920 SAGITTARIUS /
  30.1 CAPRICORN
1921 PISCES / 15.2 ARIES
1922 CAPRICORN / 25.1 AQUARIUS /
  18.2 PISCES
1923 SAGITTARIUS / 7.2 CAPRICORN
1924 PISCES / 13.2 ARIES
1925 CAPRICORN / 9.2 AQUARIUS
1926 AQUARIUS
1927 AQUARIUS / 2.2 PISCES
1928 SAGITTARIUS /
  29.1 CAPRICORN
1929 PISCES / 14.2 ARIES
1930 CAPRICORN / 25.1 AQUARIUS /
  18.2 PISCES
1931 SAGITTARIUS / 6.2 CAPRICORN
1932 PISCES / 13.2 ARIES
1933 CAPRICORN / 8.2 AQUARIUS
1934 AQUARIUS
1935 AQUARIUS / 2.2 PISCES
1936 SAGITTARIUS /
  29.1 CAPRICORN
1937 PISCES / 13.2 ARIES
1938 CAPRICORN / 24.1 AQUARIUS /
  17.2 PISCES
1939 SAGITTARIUS / 6.2 CAPRICORN
1940 PISCES / 12.2 ARIES
1941 CAPRICORN / 8.2 AQUARIUS
1942 AQUARIUS
1943 AQUARIUS / 1.2 PISCES
1944 SAGITTARIUS /
  28.1 CAPRICORN
1945 PISCES / 12.2 ARIES
1946 CAPRICORN / 24.1 AQUARIUS /
  17.2 PISCES
1947 SAGITTARIUS / 6.2 CAPRICORN
1948 PISCES / 12.2 ARIES
1949 CAPRICORN / 7.2 AQUARIUS
1950 AQUARIUS
1951 AQUARIUS / 1.2 PISCES
1952 SAGITTARIUS /
  27.1 CAPRICORN
1953 PISCES / 11.2 ARIES
1954 CAPRICORN / 23.1 AQUARIUS /
  16.2 PISCES
1955 SAGITTARIUS / 6.2 CAPRICORN
1956 PISCES / 11.2 ARIES
1957 CAPRICORN / 7.2 AQUARIUS
1958 AQUARIUS
1959 AQUARIUS / 31.1 PISCES
1960 SAGITTARIUS /
  27.1 CAPRICORN

1961 PISCES / 9.2 ARIES
1962 CAPRICORN / 23.1 AQUARIUS /
  15.2 PISCES
1963 SAGITTARIUS / 6.2 CAPRICORN
1964 PISCES / 11.2 ARIES
1965 CAPRICORN / 6.2 AQUARIUS
1966 AQUARIUS
1967 AQUARIUS / 30.1 PISCES
1968 SAGITTARIUS /
  26.1 CAPRICORN
1969 PISCES / 7.2 ARIES
1970 CAPRICORN / 22.1 AQUARIUS /
  15.2 PISCES
1971 SAGITTARIUS / 5.2 CAPRICORN
1972 PISCES / 10.2 ARIES
1973 CAPRICORN / 5.2 AQUARIUS
1974 AQUARIUS / 7.2 CAPRICORN
1975 AQUARIUS / 30.1 PISCES
1976 SAGITTARIUS /
  26.1 CAPRICORN
1977 PISCES / 5.2 ARIES
1978 CAPRICORN / 22.1 AQUARIUS /
  14.2 PISCES
1979 SAGITTARIUS / 5.2 CAPRICORN
1980 PISCES / 10.2 ARIES
1981 CAPRICORN / 5.2 AQUARIUS
1982 AQUARIUS / 29.1 CAPRICORN
1983 AQUARIUS / 29.1 PISCES
1984 SAGITTARIUS /
  25.1 CAPRICORN
1985 PISCES / 5.2 ARIES
1986 AQUARIUS / 14.2 PISCES
1987 SAGITTARIUS / 5.2 CAPRICORN
1988 PISCES / 9.2 ARIES
1989 CAPRICORN / 4.2 AQUARIUS
1990 AQUARIUS / 23.1 CAPRICORN
1991 AQUARIUS / 29.1 PISCES
1992 SAGITTARIUS /
  25.1 CAPRICORN
1993 PISCES / 4.2 ARIES
1994 AQUARIUS / 13.2 PISCES
1995 SAGITTARIUS / 5.2 CAPRICORN
1996 PISCES / 9.2 ARIES
1997 CAPRICORN / 4.2 AQUARIUS
1998 AQUARIUS / 23.1 CAPRICORN
1999 AQUARIUS / 29.1 PISCES
2000 SAGITTARIUS /
  25.1 CAPRICORN
2001 PISCES / 4.2 ARIES
2002 AQUARIUS / 13.2 PISCES
2003 SAGITTARIUS
2004 PISCES / 9.2 AQUARIUS
2005 CAPRICORN / 6.2 AQUARIUS
2006 AQUARIUS / 14.1 CAPRICORN
2007 AQUARIUS / 29.1 PISCES
2008 SAGITTARIUS / 25.1 CAPRICORN
2009 PISCES / 4.2 ARIES
2010 AQUARIUS / 12.2 PISCES

VENUS THROUGH THE ZODIAC SIGNS

Venus in Aries

Amongst other things, the position of Venus in Aries indicates a fondness for travel, music and all creative pursuits. Your nature tends to be affectionate and you would try not to create confusion or difficulty for others if it could be avoided. Many people with this planetary position have a great love of the theatre, and mental stimulation is of the greatest importance. Early romantic attachments are common with Venus in Aries, so it is very important to establish a genuine sense of romantic continuity. Early marriage is not recommended, especially if it is based on sympathy. You may give your heart a little too readily on occasions.

Venus in Taurus

You are capable of very deep feelings and your emotions tend to last for a very long time. This makes you a trusting partner and lover, whose constancy is second to none. In life you are precise and careful and always try to do things the right way. Although this means an ordered life, which you are comfortable with, it can also lead you to be rather too fussy for your own good. Despite your pleasant nature, you are very fixed in your opinions and quite able to speak your mind. Others are attracted to you and historical astrologers always quoted this position of Venus as being very fortunate in terms of marriage. However, if you find yourself involved in a failed relationship, it could take you a long time to trust again.

Venus in Gemini

As with all associations related to Gemini, you tend to be quite versatile, anxious for change and intelligent in your dealings with the world at large. You may gain money from more than one source but you are equally good at spending it. There is an inference here that you are a good communicator, via either the written or the spoken word, and you love to be in the company of interesting people. Always on the look-out for culture, you may also be very fond of music, and love to indulge the curious and cultured side of your nature. In romance you tend to have more than one relationship and could find yourself associated with someone who has previously been a friend or even a distant relative.

Venus in Cancer

You often stay close to home because you are very fond of family and enjoy many of your most treasured moments when you are with those you love. Being naturally sympathetic, you will always do anything you can to support those around you, even people you hardly know at all. This charitable side of your nature is your most noticeable trait and is one of the reasons why others are naturally so fond of you. Being receptive and in some cases even psychic, you can see through to the soul of most of those with whom you come into contact. You may not commence too many romantic attachments but when you do give your heart, it tends to be unconditionally.

Venus in Leo

It must become quickly obvious to almost anyone you meet that you are kind, sympathetic and yet determined enough to stand up for anyone or anything that is truly important to you. Bright and sunny, you warm the world with your natural enthusiasm and would rarely do anything to hurt those around you, or at least not intentionally. In romance you are ardent and sincere, though some may find your style just a little overpowering. Gains come through your contacts with other people and this could be especially true with regard to romance, for love and money often come hand in hand for those who were born with Venus in Leo. People claim to understand you, though you are more complex than you seem.

Venus in Virgo

Your nature could well be fairly quiet no matter what your Sun sign might be, though this fact often manifests itself as an inner peace and would not prevent you from being basically sociable. Some delays and even the odd disappointment in love cannot be ruled out with this planetary position, though it's a fact that you will usually find the happiness you look for in the end. Catapulting yourself into romantic entanglements that you know to be rather ill-advised is not sensible, and it would be better to wait before you committed yourself exclusively to any one person. It is the essence of your nature to serve the world at large and through doing so it is possible that you will attract money at some stage in your life.

Venus in Libra

Venus is very comfortable in Libra and bestows upon those people who have this planetary position a particular sort of kindness that is easy to recognise. This is a very good position for all sorts of friendships and also for romantic attachments that usually bring much joy into your life. Few individuals with Venus in Libra would avoid marriage and since you are capable of great depths of love, it is likely that you will find a contented personal life. You like to mix with people of integrity and intelligence but don't take kindly to scruffy surroundings or work that means getting your hands too dirty. Careful speculation, good business dealings and money through marriage all seem fairly likely.

Venus in Scorpio

You are quite open and tend to spend money quite freely, even on those occasions when you don't have very much. Although your intentions are always good, there are times when you get yourself in to the odd scrape and this can be particularly true when it comes to romance, which you may come to late or from a rather unexpected direction. Certainly you have the power to be happy and to make others contented on the way, but you find the odd stumbling block on your journey through life and it could seem that you have to work harder than those around you. As a result of this, you gain a much deeper understanding of the true value of personal happiness than many people ever do, and are likely to achieve true contentment in the end.

Venus in Sagittarius

You are lighthearted, cheerful and always able to see the funny side of any situation. These facts enhance your popularity, which is especially high with members of the opposite sex. You should never have to look too far to find romantic interest in your life, though it is just possible that you might be too willing to commit yourself before you are certain that the person in question is right for you. Part of the problem here extends to other areas of life too. The fact is that you like variety in everything and so can tire of situations that fail to offer it. All the same, if you choose wisely and learn to understand your restless side, then great happiness can be yours.

Venus in Capricorn

The most notable trait that comes from Venus in this position is that it makes you trustworthy and able to take on all sorts of responsibilities in life. People are instinctively fond of you and love you all the more because you are always ready to help those who are in any form of need. Social and business popularity can be yours and there is a magnetic quality to your nature that is particularly attractive in a romantic sense. Anyone who wants a partner for a lover, a spouse and a good friend too would almost certainly look in your direction. Constancy is the hallmark of your nature and unfaithfulness would go right against the grain. You might sometimes be a little too trusting.

Venus in Aquarius

This location of Venus offers a fondness for travel and a desire to try out something new at every possible opportunity. You are extremely easy to get along with and tend to have many friends from varied backgrounds, classes and inclinations. You like to live a distinct sort of life and gain a great deal from moving about, both in a career sense and with regard to your home. It is not out of the question that you could form a romantic attachment to someone who comes from far away or be attracted to a person of a distinctly artistic and original nature. What you cannot stand is jealousy, for you have friends of both sexes and would want to keep things that way.

Venus in Pisces

The first thing people tend to notice about you is your wonderful, warm smile. Being very charitable by nature you will do anything to help others, even if you don't know them well. Much of your life may be spent sorting out situations for other people, but it is very important to feel that you are living for yourself too. In the main, you remain cheerful, and tend to be quite attractive to members of the opposite sex. Where romantic attachments are concerned, you could be drawn to people who are significantly older or younger than yourself or to someone with a unique career or point of view. It might be best for you to avoid marrying whilst you are still very young.

THE ASTRAL DIARY

HOW THE DIAGRAMS WORK

Through the picture diagrams in the Astral Diary I want to help you to plot your year. With them you can see where the positive and negative aspects will be found in each month. To make the most of them, all you have to do is remember where and when!

Let me show you how they work ...

THE MONTH AT A GLANCE

Just as there are twelve separate zodiac signs, so astrologers believe that each sign has twelve separate aspects to life. Each of the twelve segments relates to a different personal aspect. I list them all every month so that their meanings are always clear.

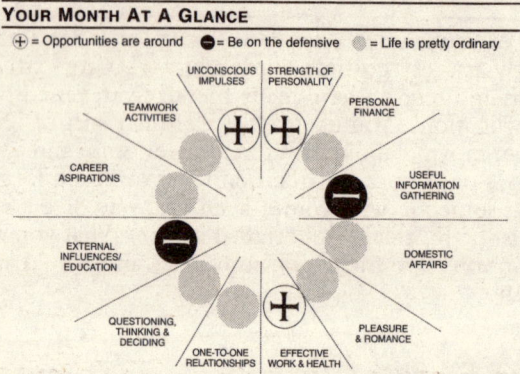

YOUR MONTH AT A GLANCE

⊕ = Opportunities are around   ⊖ = Be on the defensive   ○ = Life is pretty ordinary

UNCONSCIOUS IMPULSES
STRENGTH OF PERSONALITY
TEAMWORK ACTIVITIES
PERSONAL FINANCE
CAREER ASPIRATIONS
USEFUL INFORMATION GATHERING
EXTERNAL INFLUENCES/ EDUCATION
DOMESTIC AFFAIRS
QUESTIONING, THINKING & DECIDING
PLEASURE & ROMANCE
ONE-TO-ONE RELATIONSHIPS
EFFECTIVE WORK & HEALTH

I have designed this chart to show you how and when these twelve different aspects are being influenced throughout the year. When there is a shaded circle, nothing out of the ordinary is to be expected. However, when a circle turns white with a plus sign, the influence is positive. Where the circle is black with a minus sign, it is a negative.

YOUR ENERGY RHYTHM CHART

On the opposite page is a picture diagram in which I am linking your zodiac group to the rhythm of the Moon. In doing this I have calculated when you will be gaining strength from its influence and equally when you may be weakened by it.

If you think of yourself as being like the tides of the ocean then you may understand how your own energies must also rise and fall. And if you understand how it works and when it is working, then you can better organise your activities to achieve more and get things done more easily.

YOUR ENERGY RHYTHM CHART

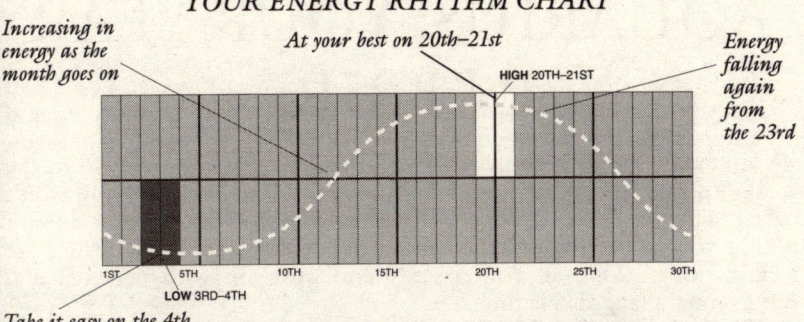

Increasing in energy as the month goes on

At your best on 20th–21st

HIGH 20TH–21ST

Energy falling again from the 23rd

LOW 3RD–4TH

Take it easy on the 4th

MOVING PICTURE SCREEN
Love, money, career and vitality measured every week

The diagram at the end of each week is designed to be informative and fun. The arrows move up and down the scale to give you an idea of the strength of your opportunities in each area. If LOVE stands at plus 4, then get out and put yourself about because things are going your way in romance! The further down the arrow goes, the weaker the opportunities. Do note that the diagram is an overall view of your astrological aspects and therefore reflects a trend which may not concur with every day in that cycle.

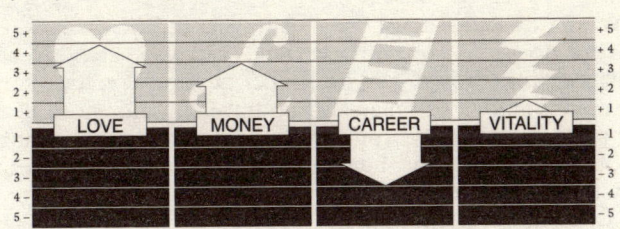

LOVE   MONEY   CAREER   VITALITY

AND FINALLY:

am ....

pm ....

The two lines that are left blank in each daily entry of the Astral Diary are for your own personal use. You may find them ideal for keeping a check on birthdays or appointments, though it could be an idea to make notes from the astrological trends and diagrams a few weeks in advance. Some of the lines are marked with a key, which indicates the working of astrological cycles in your life. Look out for them each week as they are the best days to take action or make decisions. The daily text tells you which area of your life to focus on.

☿ = Mercury is retrograde on that day.

AQUARIUS: YOUR YEAR IN BRIEF

Aquarius is in for a really positive sort of year and it starts from the word go. January and February are really your time and you won't have much chance to get bored. Others despise the winter, but it doesn't bother you in the slightest, which means you prosper while others are feeling down. Take all your energy and push on with personal and professional plans at this time.

March and April should find you coasting along nicely, with plenty of help available from the direction of colleagues and friends, together with an extra-special incentive on the romantic scene. Finances could be fairly strong at this time, or at the very least you are using what you have to the best of your ability. New moves at work could be providential now.

With the arrival of the early summer, May and June look as though they will offer you many new incentives and the ability to 'get it right' first time on a number of different occasions. You won't lack originality or enterprise and you seem to be able to persuade people to do more or less anything you choose. Family members could be argumentative around this time and you will have to be super-diplomatic in some situations.

Look to July and August for making significant changes, especially around your home. However, these trends can also extend to your work and it may seem as though you no sooner get one alteration sorted than another comes along. You may also be travelling a great deal more and this will please you because you love to be on the move. Finances could be variable around this time, but your love life can be as secure and happy as at any time throughout the year.

Along comes the autumn, and September and October may bring certain small restrictions that look as though they are going to slow you down. Nothing could be further from the truth because what they really do is to give you even more determination and a greater 'push' towards your cherished objectives. Help is on hand when you need it, though you probably won't for much of the time.

The last two months of the year, November and December, seem to offer a concentration of possibilities. It's true that you may have to be extremely sensitive to others early on, but later you can be yourself and you can socialise better than would normally be the case. The Christmas period should be filled with happiness and surprises. Your nature now turns very gregarious, but of course there is nothing remotely strange about that. What really shows more than anything now is your overwhelming and disarming originality.

January 2010

YOUR MONTH AT A GLANCE

⊕ = Opportunities are around   ⊖ = Be on the defensive   ⬤ = Life is pretty ordinary

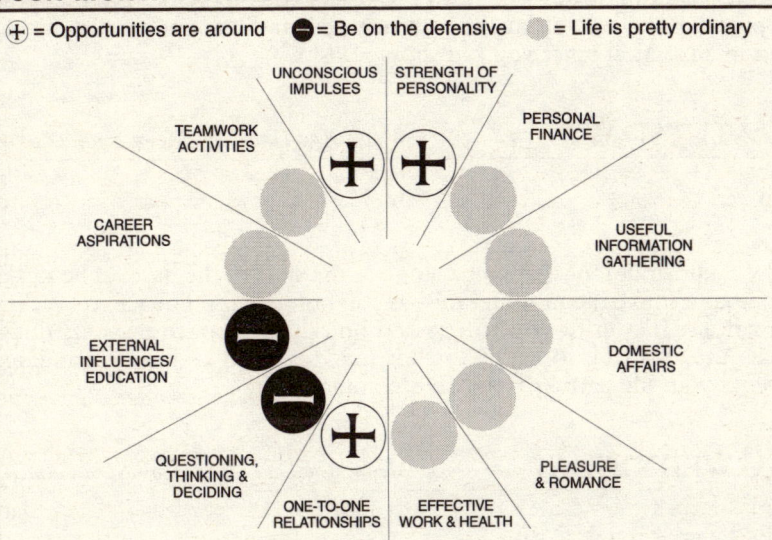

JANUARY HIGHS AND LOWS

Here I show you how the rhythms of the Moon will affect you this month. Like the tide, your energies and abilities will rise and fall with its pattern. When it is above the centre line, go for it, when it is below, you should be resting.

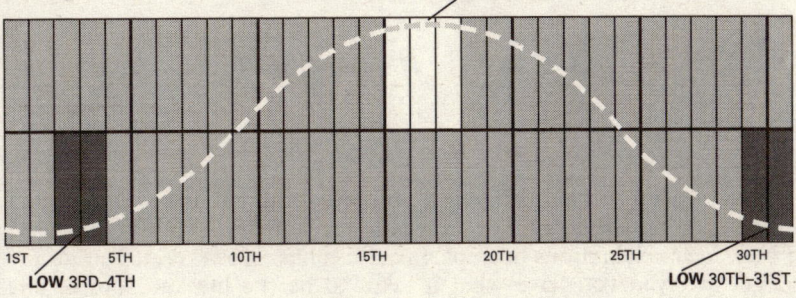

28 MONDAY

Moon Age Day 12   Moon Sign Taurus

am . . . .

pm . . . .
Venus is in the twelfth house of your solar chart, along with the Sun and Venus. This supports a reflective approach and even encourages you to withdraw from issues you don't care for the look of. As the year approaches its end you might be rather pessimistic about certain things, but in a practical sense you can show realism.

29 TUESDAY

Moon Age Day 13   Moon Sign Taurus

am . . . .

pm . . . .
Any slight irritations that come along at the start of the day can be made to disappear like the morning mist as you bring your influence to bear on situations. It's up to you to respond quickly and positively, something that Aquarius can do easily. Friends may be warm and understanding, even if your life partner is not so accommodating.

30 WEDNESDAY

Moon Age Day 14   Moon Sign Gemini

am . . . .

pm . . . .
This may not be the best time to engage in strenuous activities, because you could be more susceptible to strains and sprains than would normally be the case. At the same time you might feel you have socialised enough to last half a lifetime, and there is much to be said for slowing things down socially. Why not try a new game or pastime today?

31 THURSDAY

Moon Age Day 15   Moon Sign Gemini

am . . . .

pm . . . .
The benevolent and understanding aspects of your nature are emphasised today, assisting you to gain popularity in most circles. Don't be surprised if New Year celebrations prompt mixed feelings. However, if you decide to get involved you have what it takes to be the life and soul of any occasion and to see in the New Year happily.

1 FRIDAY
☿   *Moon Age Day 16   Moon Sign Cancer*

am . . . .

pm . . . .
The start of the year coincides with a key period during which you need to look again at some of your most important plans. It might be necessary to change your direction significantly, but you can take this in your stride. By all means seek assistance from relatives and friends, and be prepared to respond if you get more than you bargained for!

2 SATURDAY
☿   *Moon Age Day 17   Moon Sign Cancer*

am . . . .

pm . . . .
Getting on in quite the way you wish might be difficult for a few days. By this afternoon the Moon will have entered the sign of Leo, bringing that part of the month known as the lunar low. This does little to assist your efforts to get exactly what you want from life, though it's still important to retain your usual optimism.

3 SUNDAY
☿   *Moon Age Day 18   Moon Sign Leo*

am . . . .

pm . . . .
Life could seem like hard work today, even if you are not working at all. It might feel as though a combination of winter weather, post-Christmas blues and the lunar low are ganging up on you right now. You can afford to let others take the strain while you kick off your shoes and put your feet up. Now is a time for planning rather than doing.

	LOVE	MONEY	CAREER	VITALITY
5 +				+ 5
4 +				+ 4
3 +				+ 3
2 +				+ 2
1 +				+ 1
1 −				− 1
2 −				− 2
3 −				− 3
4 −				− 4
5 −				− 5

4 MONDAY ☿ *Moon Age Day 19 Moon Sign Leo*

am . . . .

pm . . . .
Today's challenges come through personal relationships and the way you approach all sorts of associations with other people. If it appears that not everyone is on your side at the moment, your best response is to be more accommodating than ever – or end up having rows! There is much to be said for carrying on in your own sweet way.

5 TUESDAY ☿ *Moon Age Day 20 Moon Sign Virgo*

am . . . .

pm . . . .
Many of the significant events that are on offer around you at this time have a spiritual dimension. This is partly linked to the position of Mercury in your solar twelfth house, which also allows you to explain your innermost feelings much better. Your sensitivity is enhanced, and you can use it to understand others.

6 WEDNESDAY ☿ *Moon Age Day 21 Moon Sign Virgo*

am . . . .

pm . . . .
Partnerships function best if you are able to avoid extremes of any kind, either in attitude or actions. Stay middle of the road in your plans and co-operate as much as possible with your opposite number. This is just as important in a business partnership as it is in a romantic one. This is no time to be going off at an Aquarian tangent.

7 THURSDAY ☿ *Moon Age Day 22 Moon Sign Libra*

am . . . .

pm . . . .
With the Sun now in your solar twelfth house there may be a slight tendency for you to retreat into your own little world. There can be a positive side to this, because it offers you a chance to think about things more deeply and to arrive at some positive conclusions. All the same, you need to avoid making it harder for others to approach you.

8 FRIDAY   ☿   *Moon Age Day 23   Moon Sign Libra*

am . . . .

pm . . . .
The spotlight is on your deep desire to succeed at the moment, especially where work is concerned. What you are able to get out of life around now is directly proportional to the amount of effort you are willing to put in. Confidence should remain essentially high if you are taking on challenges you have chosen yourself, or at least understand well.

9 SATURDAY   ☿   *Moon Age Day 24   Moon Sign Scorpio*

am . . . .

pm . . . .
Relationships will probably respond best now if you keep the dominant and argumentative side of your nature under wraps. Mars is in your solar seventh house, doing little to help you to co-operate with others. For the moment a quite critical trend is evident, and you may not take kindly to being told how things should be done.

10 SUNDAY   ☿   *Moon Age Day 25   Moon Sign Scorpio*

am . . . .

pm . . . .
The Sun in your solar twelfth house encourages you to spend more time than usual in your own little world. Aquarius is generally a very gregarious zodiac sign and people are probably used to you being out there with the talkers. Bear in mind that you have the potential to surprise your friends if you are now more inclined to listen.

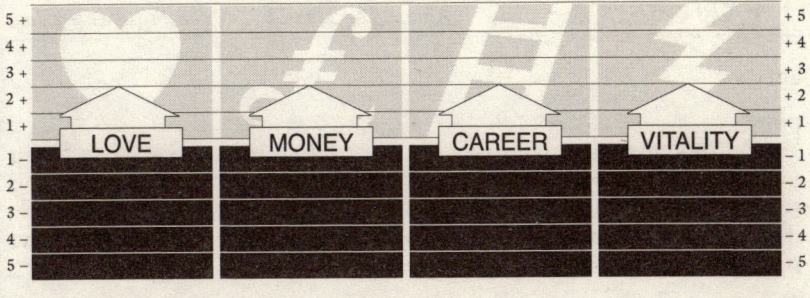

11 MONDAY ☿ *Moon Age Day 26 Moon Sign Sagittarius*

am . . . .

pm . . . .
The position of the Moon now assists you to be slightly more sociable at
the start of this week and to mix more freely than might have been the
case during the weekend. This would also be an ideal time to get yourself
a bargain, so perhaps you should be looking at the January sales. Working
with close associates is well accented.

12 TUESDAY ☿ *Moon Age Day 27 Moon Sign Sagittarius*

am . . . .

pm . . . .
Being true to yourself does not necessarily mean having to compromise
with others all the time. You can follow your own thoughts and let those
around you know the way you are thinking, whether or not they choose
to follow suit. In the end many of your present hunches could turn out
to be more or less correct.

13 WEDNESDAY ☿ *Moon Age Day 28 Moon Sign Sagittarius*

am . . . .

pm . . . .
There's nothing wrong with indulging your imagination today – and
indeed for the remainder of the week. Working out how things might
happen 'if' can be fun, even if you never actually get the chance to try.
None of this need prevent the practical side of your nature from taking
over when there are real jobs to be done.

14 THURSDAY ☿ *Moon Age Day 29 Moon Sign Capricorn*

am . . . .

pm . . . .
Your competitive nature is easily stimulated now, urging you to try to get
your own way in most situations. Whether you can actually achieve this
remains to be seen, but bear in mind that a sense of annoyance is possible
if you sense your will is being blocked. At home you have what it takes
to maintain harmony in relationships.

15 FRIDAY ☿ *Moon Age Day 0   Moon Sign Capricorn*

am . . . .

pm . . . .

If you don't set limits right now about the amount you are willing to help others, you could find that you are being taken for granted. By all means do what you can to be of assistance, but remember that you have your own life to live too. It ought to be possible to reach out to others without feeling you have become a doormat.

16 SATURDAY ☿ *Moon Age Day 1   Moon Sign Aquarius*

am . . . .

pm . . . .

Prepare yourself for a few pleasant surprises today. The Moon has now moved into your own zodiac sign and that means that for the next few days you can capitalise on that period known as the lunar high. By avoiding negative states of mind you can take advantage of a potentially dynamic and fortunate phase.

17 SUNDAY *Moon Age Day 2   Moon Sign Aquarius*

am . . . .

pm . . . .

Today offers an opportunity to make real progress and to concentrate your efforts on movement and activity. This is an ideal time to put yourself about and to make the most of the chance to become flavour of the month in a social sense. When it comes to romance, you can afford to show just how attractive you can be.

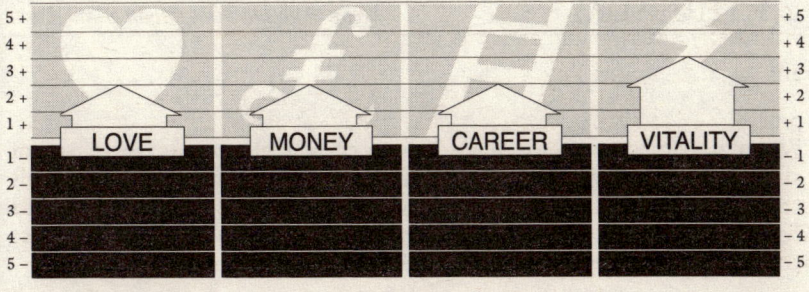

18 MONDAY

Moon Age Day 3   Moon Sign Aquarius

am . . . .

pm . . . .
As you start a new working week the Moon remains in Aquarius, encouraging you to take a determined and dynamic approach. Your strength now lies in your willingness to seek out and accept any extra responsibility that is available. An ideal day to get to know people who have been strangers up to now and turn them into new friends.

19 TUESDAY

Moon Age Day 4   Moon Sign Pisces

am . . . .

pm . . . .
You now have scope to make your social and romantic life more interesting, and with Venus in your first house romance is also well marked. Even the winter weather, which might upset others, needn't deter you from seeking to make the most of this fascinating period. Very little should prevent you from getting on well this week.

20 WEDNESDAY

Moon Age Day 5   Moon Sign Pisces

am . . . .

pm . . . .
In close partnerships it may be difficult to be tolerant of the beliefs of others, which is most unlike you. This is a very short trend and is linked to the position of the Moon. Your best response is not to take decisive actions today and avoid reacting to things that would normally go over your head. It might be better to spend time alone than to argue.

21 THURSDAY

Moon Age Day 6   Moon Sign Aries

am . . . .

pm . . . .
When it comes to major negotiations of just about any sort, paying attention is the key. Rather than taking things for granted, it's worth checking and re-checking appointments and arrangements to avoid complications later. Newer and better financial opportunities are on offer, and might begin to show themselves at any time.

22 FRIDAY
Moon Age Day 7   Moon Sign Aries

am ....

pm ....
You have what it takes to score some significant successes at the moment, and shouldn't be too put out if you have to alter your ideas at a moment's notice. It's a question of taking life very much in your stride, and as a result showing yourself to the world at large more like a typical Aquarian should.

23 SATURDAY
Moon Age Day 8   Moon Sign Aries

am ....

pm ....
Any slight setbacks may be related to the planet Mars, which could make romantic relationships a little more difficult than usual. Misunderstandings are possible, and you might not be able to get your opposite number to toe the line in the way you would wish. A great deal of understanding and a degree of psychology is now necessary.

24 SUNDAY
Moon Age Day 9   Moon Sign Taurus

am ....

pm ....
Pleasure pursuits are now positively highlighted, and with Venus in your solar first house you needn't allow that cranky position of Mars to matter too much. There is now an opportunity to make definite progress with romantic matters, and you can afford to feel free and energetic in most circumstances. Family ties are emphasised.

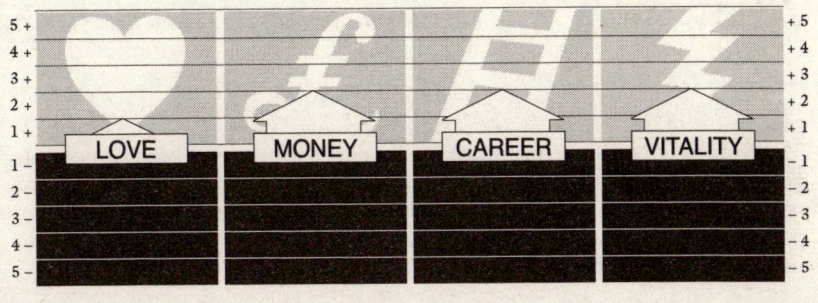

25 MONDAY
Moon Age Day 10   Moon Sign Taurus

am . . . .

pm . . . .
There are good reasons to be bold and ambitious, something that hasn't really been the case too much during January. If you feel as if life has just been ticking over for you, suddenly it's time to get yourself in gear. You have scope to be at your most effective when you are among people who stimulate your imagination.

26 TUESDAY
Moon Age Day 11   Moon Sign Gemini

am . . . .

pm . . . .
Feelings now run close to the surface in a personal sense, and it may be difficult to avoid showing others what you feel about them. In a general sense a more easygoing approach is possible, and this assists you to remain popular with colleagues and friends. However, there may still be the odd person that you can't get on with at any price.

27 WEDNESDAY
Moon Age Day 12   Moon Sign Gemini

am . . . .

pm . . . .
Be prepared to express yourself with grace and style today, and especially this evening. Everything in your world should now be harmonious, and if it isn't, you should be doing your very best to make it so. Positive feelings predominate and you know very well how to get others to do your bidding under almost any circumstance.

28 THURSDAY
Moon Age Day 13   Moon Sign Cancer

am . . . .

pm . . . .
The Sun has now moved on into your solar first house – the best possible position, because that means it is in Aquarius. Don't be afraid to be motivated by your ambitions, and be willing to try new things whenever possible. Ask yourself whether it is really necessary to sideline your personal life even if you are busy in a social sense.

29 FRIDAY
Moon Age Day 14   Moon Sign Cancer

am . . . .

pm . . . .
By all means remain ready for action, especially at work, though you shouldn't expect everything to go your way. You may require some help from others in a practical sense, and might be able to get things going more smoothly by co-operating. In particular it's worth recognising that professional advice is sometimes essential.

30 SATURDAY
Moon Age Day 15   Moon Sign Leo

am . . . .

pm . . . .
A day to keep a lid on some of your emotions, because it will be difficult to gain anything now by being absolutely truthful about the way you feel. In any case, your mind could be changing all the time at the moment, and this is certainly not a good period for burning any bridges. A sluggish interlude is possible whilst the lunar low is around.

31 SUNDAY
Moon Age Day 16   Moon Sign Leo

am . . . .

pm . . . .
Certain situations may not work in the way you might have come to expect. Potential pitfalls are evident, and it could be difficult to know exactly how you should proceed. You needn't allow this to prevent progress, because problems linked to the lunar low often tend to be paper tigers. It pays to watch and wait for a day or two.

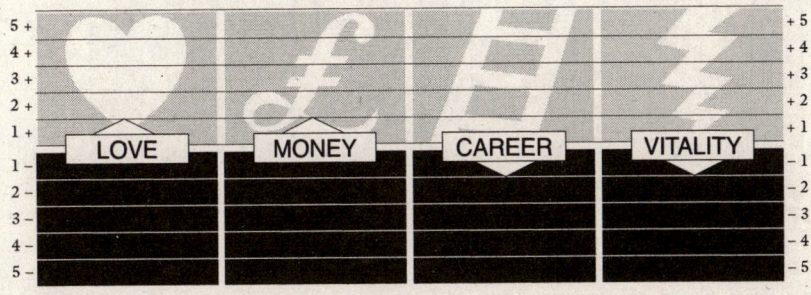

February

2010

YOUR MONTH AT A GLANCE

⊕ = Opportunities are around   ⊖ = Be on the defensive   ⬤ = Life is pretty ordinary

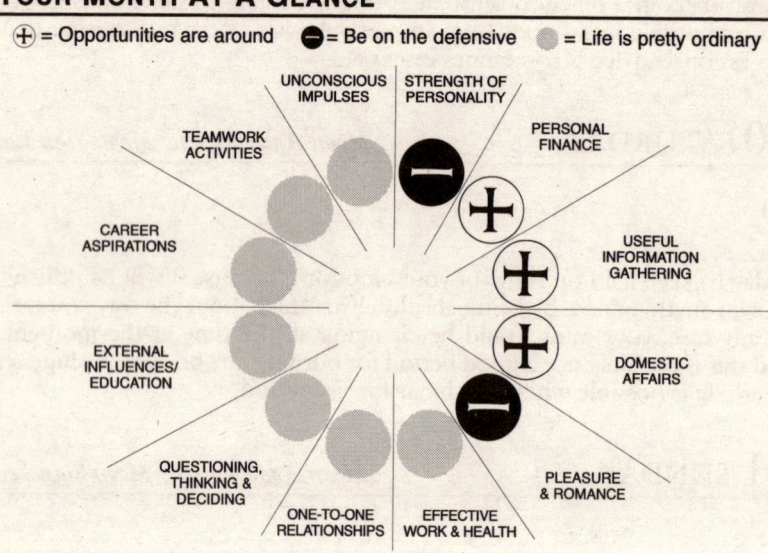

FEBRUARY HIGHS AND LOWS

Here I show you how the rhythms of the Moon will affect you this month. Like the tide, your energies and abilities will rise and fall with its pattern. When it is above the centre line, go for it, when it is below, you should be resting.

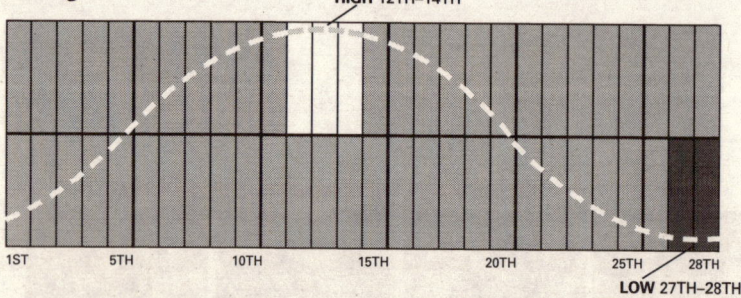

HIGH 12TH–14TH

LOW 27TH–28TH

1 MONDAY
Moon Age Day 17   Moon Sign Virgo

am . . . .

pm . . . .
The Sun is in your zodiac sign, and your personal light should be shining more brightly as a result. Energy and leadership skills are both emphasised, and you can use them to make sure people don't question your ability or your right to be out there in front. In a social sense you have everything you need to become the centre of attention.

2 TUESDAY
Moon Age Day 18   Moon Sign Virgo

am . . . .

pm . . . .
This might prove to be a key moment as far as progress of a practical sort is concerned. Any blockages that were evident during January can now be done away with altogether, and you should have an opportunity to move forward very positively as a result. If people recognise you as a winner, you can persuade them to be part of your game.

3 WEDNESDAY
Moon Age Day 19   Moon Sign Libra

am . . . .

pm . . . .
This may be one of the better days of the year so far during which you can experience a sense of personal freedom. Nothing much might have changed apart from your attitude, but that's what really matters to an Aquarian. If you believe that something is possible, you can make it so. Friends could be very accommodating at the moment.

4 THURSDAY
Moon Age Day 20   Moon Sign Libra

am . . . .

pm . . . .
Planetary trends now offer you a winning streak as far as love is concerned and you have what it takes to be extremely popular when mixing with people you know and also those you do not. Conversation comes as easy to you as breathing, and you can use your skills to talk freely to anyone, and on a host of different topics.

5 FRIDAY
Moon Age Day 21   Moon Sign Scorpio

am . . . .

pm . . . .
Daily issues, though not without setbacks, should work out more or less the way you want. Of course you can be quite dynamic at the moment, and in some respects you might be moving too quickly. There are moments today when it would be sensible to stand and stare for a while. If you act in haste you may regret the fact later.

6 SATURDAY
Moon Age Day 22   Moon Sign Scorpio

am . . . .

pm . . . .
Today's trends support a slightly argumentative interlude, though of course it's natural for you to feel that it is not you but other people who are being unreasonable. Nevertheless it takes two to tango, and if you refuse to become involved, arguments cannot take place. Be ready to make the most of social invitations later in the day.

7 SUNDAY
Moon Age Day 23   Moon Sign Scorpio

am . . . .

pm . . . .
The pace of your social life can now be quickened, and it's time to wake up even more to the opportunities that February is bringing. Today's events can provide mental stimulation, and you should be filled with a sense of anticipation regarding new plans. If family members want to have you around today, be prepared to comply!

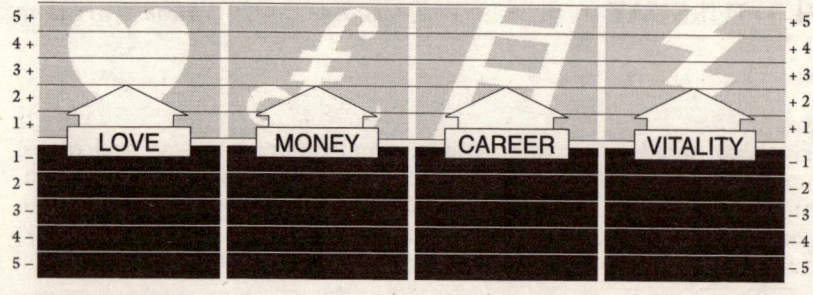

8 MONDAY
Moon Age Day 24   Moon Sign Sagittarius

am . . . .

pm . . . .
The spotlight is now on your heart-felt approach to others, and the way you treat them is a mark of respect to the sort of individual you are. Nothing seems to be too much trouble, and you should be happy to put yourself out for a good cause. Ensuring that you are good to have around can help you to inspire others on to greater things.

9 TUESDAY
Moon Age Day 25   Moon Sign Sagittarius

am . . . .

pm . . . .
The time is right to follow your heart, especially as far as relationships are concerned. You can be self-motivated at the moment and have tremendous inner strength, which is why you can achieve almost anything you set out to do. At work it is possible that rules and regulations might get in the way, but there are ways round them.

10 WEDNESDAY
Moon Age Day 26   Moon Sign Capricorn

am . . . .

pm . . . .
Putting others first is part of your nature, but this tendency is especially well marked under present planetary trends. In particular you can afford to show great concern for anyone who is in trouble and to put yourself out to help. This is a favourable time to focus on family matters and for getting involved in group discussions.

11 THURSDAY
Moon Age Day 27   Moon Sign Capricorn

am . . . .

pm . . . .
Look to achieve a change for the better as far as your love life is concerned, especially if things have been a little topsy-turvy of late. Make the most of opportunities to form new friendships, and to come face to face with people you find socially and even personally attractive.

12 FRIDAY
Moon Age Day 28   Moon Sign Aquarius

am . . . .

pm . . . .

An optimistic attitude can go a very long way now that the lunar high has arrived. It's time to get Lady Luck on your side and be willing to take more chances than you usually would. Why not get out to the shops if possible and look for a bargain or two? In a social sense you can afford to take centre stage and boost your popularity in the process.

13 SATURDAY
Moon Age Day 29   Moon Sign Aquarius

am . . . .

pm . . . .

Getting your own way with others shouldn't be difficult now. You can continue to take chances, though these are probably of a calculated sort because you are also quite careful under present planetary trends. Wherever you look today you can find scope for interest and advancement. Your cheerful nature should be there for all to see.

14 SUNDAY
Moon Age Day 0   Moon Sign Aquarius

am . . . .

pm . . . .

Even if your ability to communicate with others is always good, at the moment it could be positively legendary! It doesn't matter what sort of people you are associating with, what does matter is your willingness to adapt your own nature to suit theirs. You might decide that this Sunday would be a favourable time to take a trip.

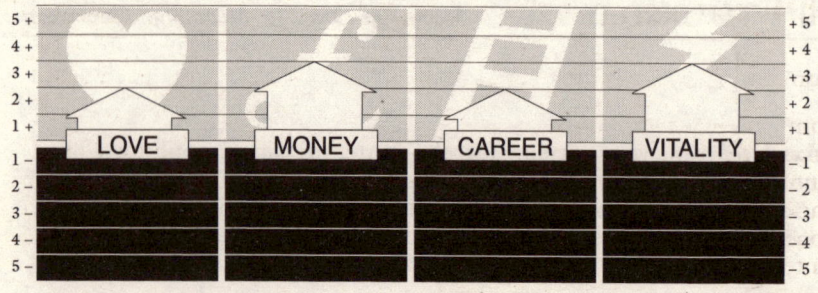

15 MONDAY

Moon Age Day 1   Moon Sign Pisces

am . . . .

pm . . . .
One-to-one relationships might seem slightly downbeat at the present time, and you will need to be fairly tactful and understanding if you are to retain the closeness that you cherish. You needn't worry too much, because it is impossible for people to see eye-to-eye all the time. Remember that others may be subject to stresses you aren't aware of.

16 TUESDAY

Moon Age Day 2   Moon Sign Pisces

am . . . .

pm . . . .
Mercury is now in your solar second house and you can use this trend to make the best of financial matters. The emphasis is on possessions and the way you view them, and on how careful you decide to be when it comes to spending your cash. You might decide to sell something of worth that is no longer of any real use to you.

17 WEDNESDAY

Moon Age Day 3   Moon Sign Aries

am . . . .

pm . . . .
Despite positive financial influences, you would be wise to show a degree of common sense when it comes to buying luxury items right now. If you choose to look around instead of opting for the first thing you see, it might be possible to get a real bargain. At work an inventive approach can assist you to achieve success around now.

18 THURSDAY

Moon Age Day 4   Moon Sign Aries

am . . . .

pm . . . .
You are best suited today to being where the action is, so being shoved into some corner to work quietly wouldn't be ideal. If you want to be noticed, there's nothing wrong with pushing yourself forward whenever possible. In social situations it's time to show just how charming and intellectual you can be, and to gain admirers as a result.

19 FRIDAY

Moon Age Day 5   Moon Sign Aries

am . . . .

pm . . . .
You can now afford to be very warm and supportive to your friends and approachable to strangers too. There is a private side to your nature that is significant at present, and this is emphasised by the present position of the Moon. This may seem slightly at odds with the more gregarious side of your nature, which is also highlighted now.

20 SATURDAY

Moon Age Day 6   Moon Sign Taurus

am . . . .

pm . . . .
A certain degree of caution would be no bad thing, particularly if you have strong views to express. It pays to avoid needless arguments, if necessary by taking yourself right away from specific situations. It's fine to hold very definite opinions, though bear in mind that these might clash with those of equally determined and self-assured types.

21 SUNDAY

Moon Age Day 7   Moon Sign Taurus

am . . . .

pm . . . .
There are gains to be made from building upon recent successes and looking after your finances carefully. Personal security counts for a great deal at this time, particularly in relation to your long-term financial prospects. Even if you were quite willing to take chances early in the month, there is far less encouragement to do so today.

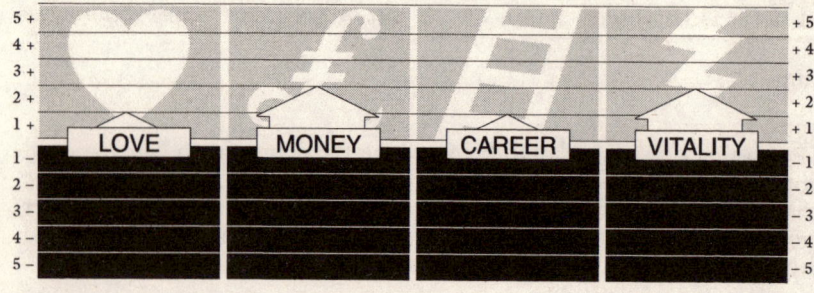

22 MONDAY
Moon Age Day 8   Moon Sign Gemini

am . . . .

pm . . . .
Creative efforts are well accented right now, and you can direct them towards making your environment, either at home or at work, as pleasant as possible for everyone concerned. You should be quite willing to co-operate, though you have potential to find your way to the front of any group and to show that it's the natural place for you to be.

23 TUESDAY
Moon Age Day 9   Moon Sign Gemini

am . . . .

pm . . . .
You have scope to thrive in situations where you can express your taste and enjoy material luxury. All the same, there's nothing wrong with being more ambitious and dynamic under present trends, and you need to ask whether you are making the most of your potential. Venus is in your second house, working favourably on your behalf.

24 WEDNESDAY
Moon Age Day 10   Moon Sign Cancer

am . . . .

pm . . . .
Dealing with your partner when they are on a short fuse can be tricky, and you need to be careful to avoid saying or doing the wrong thing. Why not let them take the lead, and be content to follow for a few hours? This might prevent you from getting things wrong. There's nothing to stop you taking command outside of personal attachments.

25 THURSDAY
Moon Age Day 11   Moon Sign Cancer

am . . . .

pm . . . .
Being properly organised is definitely the best key to success at this stage of the week. There are constant gains to be made from knowing how you are going to act under any given circumstance, and leaving things to chance is not to be recommended. New activities could now offer you the opportunity to forge new friendships.

26 FRIDAY

Moon Age Day 12   Moon Sign Cancer

am . . . .

pm . . . .
Save time later today to recharge your batteries. By this afternoon the lunar low will be coming into view and you may decide to let those around you make many of the decisions and do much of the work. Regeneration is the order of the day, and there should be less necessity to be out there doing the whole thing yourself.

27 SATURDAY

Moon Age Day 13   Moon Sign Leo

am . . . .

pm . . . .
You are right in the middle of a planetary lull, and the best way to deal with it is to admit that you can't keep moving forward at your accustomed speed. It shouldn't do you any harm at all to sit back and watch the flowers grow for a while – if you can find any flowers at this point in the year! Make the most of some valuable thinking time.

28 SUNDAY

Moon Age Day 14   Moon Sign Leo

am . . . .

pm . . . .
The time is now right to pursue money matters, but there's nothing wrong with doing so from the comfort of your own favourite chair. Even if you don't push yourself forward today, by tomorrow more powerful trends take over again and the lunar low will be gone. You may not wander far but your mind can take fantastic journeys.

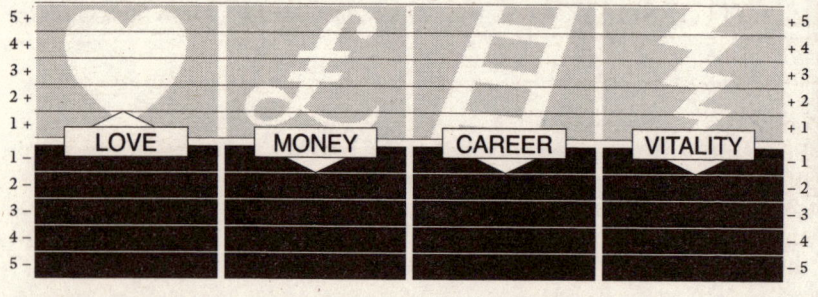

March 2010

YOUR MONTH AT A GLANCE

⊕ = Opportunities are around   ⊖ = Be on the defensive   ⬤ = Life is pretty ordinary

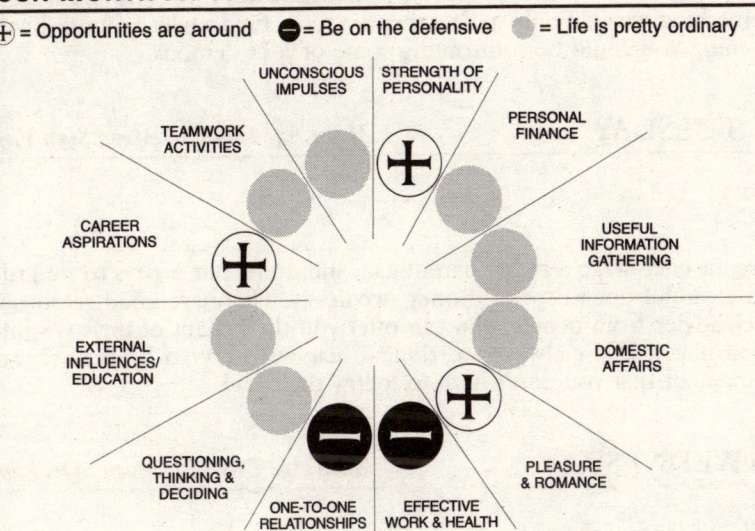

MARCH HIGHS AND LOWS

Here I show you how the rhythms of the Moon will affect you this month. Like the tide, your energies and abilities will rise and fall with its pattern. When it is above the centre line, go for it, when it is below, you should be resting.

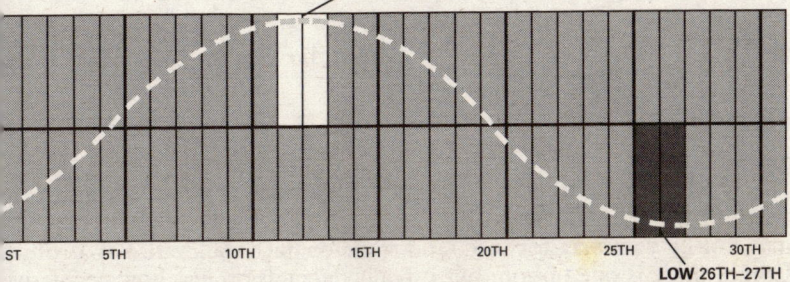

HIGH 12TH–13TH

1ST 5TH 10TH 15TH 20TH 25TH 30TH

LOW 26TH–27TH

1 MONDAY
Moon Age Day 15   Moon Sign Virgo

am . . . .

pm . . . .
Are certain matters getting rather too serious for your liking? Today
would be an ideal time to lighten things up. You might decide to
accomplish this by cheering up your friends and motivating them to do
something new – if only so that they are more fun to have around. By the
evening you could be confronting some of your demons.

2 TUESDAY
Moon Age Day 16   Moon Sign Virgo

am . . . .

pm . . . .
Trends encourage a rather extravagant interlude, but it pays to be just a
little careful not to spend money needlessly. There are good reasons to
seek advice from people who can offer you the benefit of their wisdom,
even if you don't always see things their way. Try to be patient, and
remember that you don't have to follow their lead.

3 WEDNESDAY
Moon Age Day 17   Moon Sign Libra

am . . . .

pm . . . .
A total change of scenery could suit you perfectly around now, though it
might not be very easy to arrange at short notice. You can still take
excursions in your mind and should be allowing your imagination to
work overtime around now. With everything to play for in sports and
group interests, it's time to make sure you have a full social life.

4 THURSDAY
Moon Age Day 18   Moon Sign Libra

am . . . .

pm . . . .
You would be wise to play it safe today, especially at work, and not take
anything for granted. What other people think is the best way to proceed
may not be your way forward, and some conflict could arise as a result.
Compromise is one option, but it really depends on just how persuasive
you can be. Be prepared to use a psychological approach.

5 FRIDAY
Moon Age Day 19   Moon Sign Scorpio

am . . . .

pm . . . .
Pursuing career issues is well starred now, and you can afford to be quite positive today that you know what you want from your life. Getting others to see things your way is something you should be increasingly good at, and you have what it takes to carry whole groups of people with you. Confidence needn't be lacking at this time.

6 SATURDAY
Moon Age Day 20   Moon Sign Scorpio

am . . . .

pm . . . .
This is a period during which you can capitalise on all the effort you have put in previously. In other words, if you worked hard in the past, you now deserve to reap the rewards. Others might not see things in quite this way, but you can be so persuasive at the moment that you can bring anyone round to your point of view.

7 SUNDAY
Moon Age Day 21   Moon Sign Sagittarius

am . . . .

pm . . . .
This has potential to be a fairly productive day, but it can also be frustrating, particularly if you have good ideas that you can't put into practice until tomorrow or even later in the week. Fill your mind with fun and seek out the company of stimulating people. It's a question of finding individuals whose interests mirror your own.

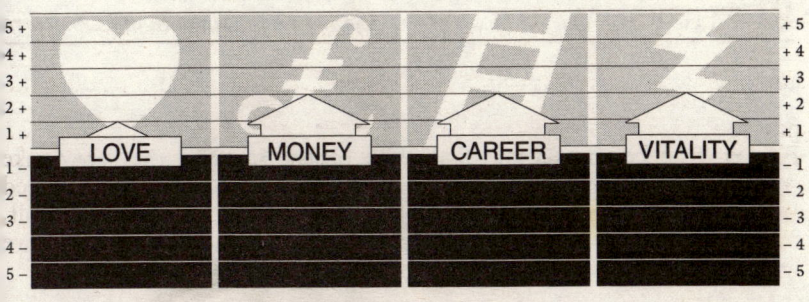

8 MONDAY
Moon Age Day 22   Moon Sign Sagittarius

am . . . .

pm . . . .
It might be slightly difficult to get your message across today, especially if it seems that people are refusing to listen. Your best approach is to keep calm, and if one method doesn't work, try another. The emphasis now is on working with people rather than with things, and on accommodating the differences you encounter around you.

9 TUESDAY
Moon Age Day 23   Moon Sign Capricorn

am . . . .

pm . . . .
You now have scope to bring greater stability to your life than of late. The Sun is presently in your solar second house, encouraging you to take care of finances and decide what direction you want to follow in life. Whether or not you can persuade other people to take the journey with you in the way you wish remains to be seen.

10 WEDNESDAY
Moon Age Day 24   Moon Sign Capricorn

am . . . .

pm . . . .
Though some aspects of your personal life might seem slightly unsettled around now, there is much to be said for soldiering on and trying to find solutions to any difficulties. Beware of overstating problems, and be ready to look for humour when you can. It's time to counter any negative thoughts with a more light-hearted view.

11 THURSDAY
Moon Age Day 25   Moon Sign Capricorn

am . . . .

pm . . . .
Is it really necessary to find fault with others, whether they are work colleagues or family members? It's natural to feel that you have all the answers at the moment, but beware because too much pride could lead to the odd fall. Confidence should remain strong when you are dealing with financial matters.

12 FRIDAY   *Moon Age Day 26   Moon Sign Aquarius*

am . . . .

pm . . . .
Make an early start and get stuck into life for all you are worth! There are
definite gains to be made, and with the lunar high around these could be
available almost as soon as you are up and about. The signs are that with
just a little effort on your part today and tomorrow you can more than
double your luck, and enjoy yourself too.

13 SATURDAY   *Moon Age Day 27   Moon Sign Aquarius*

am . . . .

pm . . . .
There is more than one way to achieve the progress you presently crave,
and what's more you can afford to rely on the good offices of others to
help you out. The weekend offers you the opportunity to get out of the
house and to enjoy good company all round. A light-hearted approach
to life still works best.

14 SUNDAY   *Moon Age Day 28   Moon Sign Pisces*

am . . . .

pm . . . .
Future prospects look especially favourable when it comes to your
personal finances, so it's worth devoting at least some time to these today.
Planning ahead is good, but making up your mind on the spur of the
moment can be equally effective, especially in a romantic and social sense.
By all means stand up for a family member who is having problems.

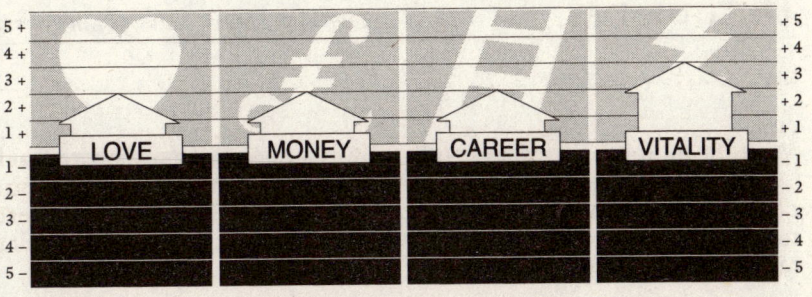

15 MONDAY

Moon Age Day 0   Moon Sign Pisces

am . . . .

pm . . . .
Personal fulfilment is now possible through successful communication. Fortunately this is not a problem for Aquarius, and you can give a good account of yourself in any company. Your classless and unpretentious approach assists you to charm the birds from the trees all day long. Don't be surprised if people actively want to have you around.

16 TUESDAY

Moon Age Day 1   Moon Sign Pisces

am . . . .

pm . . . .
This would be an ideal time to take a close look at your partner's needs and do what you can to make life easier for them. A helpful approach is possible right across the board, though you may not have much time for those who bleat about situations they could easily alter. Personal confidence should remain high between now and the weekend.

17 WEDNESDAY

Moon Age Day 2   Moon Sign Aries

am . . . .

pm . . . .
Set the tone for the day by making sure you are aware of all the new possibilities that stand around you at this time. There are positive monetary goals to approach, and you could also be on the verge of a personal success, possibly associated in some way with education. Are people looking at you with admiration? That suits you fine!

18 THURSDAY

Moon Age Day 3   Moon Sign Aries

am . . . .

pm . . . .
Make the most of a varied and potentially exciting social atmosphere that is around you at this time. Of course you should be contributing, because nobody likes to mix and mingle more than Aquarius. You might discover that you have some sort of gift that even you didn't expect. It doesn't matter how silly it might seem – it's something new.

19 FRIDAY
Moon Age Day 4   Moon Sign Taurus

am . . . .

pm . . . .
Today's major rewards can come through domestic and family involvements. Even if you are still busy out there in the wider world, when you are at home you have scope to find most happiness. Be prepared to show pride in your relatives and to sing their praises to the sky regarding their achievements this month.

20 SATURDAY
Moon Age Day 5   Moon Sign Taurus

am . . . .

pm . . . .
Keep abreast of all news and views whilst Mercury occupies your solar third house. You should know automatically when things you hear could turn out to be useful, and it pays to keep your ever-attentive mind even busier at this time. When it comes to dealing with issues that have worried you in the past, you might now wonder why they ever did.

21 SUNDAY
Moon Age Day 6   Moon Sign Taurus

am . . . .

pm . . . .
Being at the centre of things shouldn't be a problem to you now – but then again, is it ever? You have what it takes to show yourself to the world at large exactly as a good Aquarian should, and to wear your originality like a badge of honour. Take anything that is said about you with a pinch of salt, because it probably isn't intended as an insult.

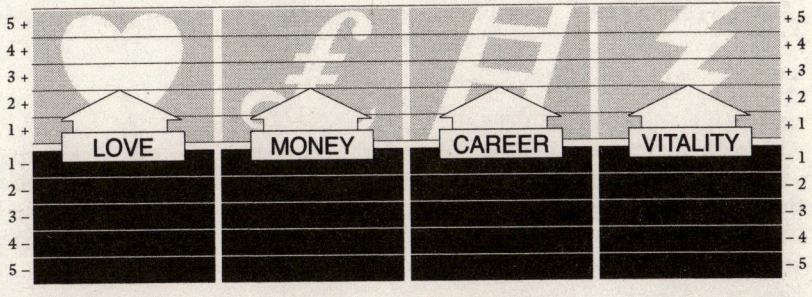

22 MONDAY
Moon Age Day 7   Moon Sign Gemini

am . . . .

pm . . . .
Today has potential to get off to a very optimistic start and there are newer and more interesting opportunities cropping up all the time. This is another of your better days for learning new things and for swapping information with colleagues and friends. All electronic forms of communication are also well highlighted at this time.

23 TUESDAY
Moon Age Day 8   Moon Sign Gemini

am . . . .

pm . . . .
Now it is the workplace that is most favoured as you strive to streamline your working life. Impressing others on the way shouldn't be at all difficult, and your innovative attitude should be there for all to see. Be prepared to give advice and support to others, particularly those who have been having problems.

24 WEDNESDAY
Moon Age Day 9   Moon Sign Cancer

am . . . .

pm . . . .
Social matters can be boosted if you are willing to bring your entertaining personality to bear on gatherings. Handling several different interests at the same time shouldn't be too much of a problem, and you can interest even the most demanding and exacting of characters. The middle of this week should be good for any form of sport.

25 THURSDAY
Moon Age Day 10   Moon Sign Cancer

am . . . .

pm . . . .
Although there are a couple of quieter days ahead, you can still keep pushing forward today. With the lunar low approaching, it's worth thinking about tying up a few loose ends, and it might not be too sensible to start awkward new jobs until the weekend. Be willing to listen to a radically different point of view at home.

26 FRIDAY
Moon Age Day 11   Moon Sign Leo

am . . . .

pm . . . .
Life might get off to a fairly slow start, and most of today could seem to
be a game of catch-up for many Aquarians. If you are able to retain your
sense of humour you shouldn't be too put out by the Moon in Leo.
There's nothing wrong with relying on the good offices of friends and
family members when it comes to getting specific jobs done.

27 SATURDAY
Moon Age Day 12   Moon Sign Leo

am . . . .

pm . . . .
Making a good impression shouldn't be difficult, even if you feel as
though you are blundering through life at the moment. This needn't be
the case at all, and even if you do show your vulnerability at this time, this
might only make others love you all the more. Your kind-hearted
approach to life has never been more welcome.

28 SUNDAY
Moon Age Day 13   Moon Sign Virgo

am . . . .

pm . . . .
Be ready to capitalise on what can be a very rewarding phase in terms of
personal relationships. Aquarians who have been looking for love should
keep their eyes wide open because they might be able to find it around
the next corner. Do your best to get things in context, especially
concerning the behaviour of younger family members.

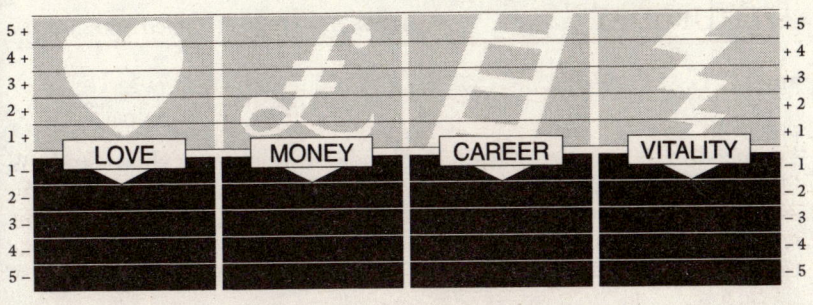

29 MONDAY
Moon Age Day 14   Moon Sign Virgo

am . . . .

pm . . . .
Look out for tension in personal relationships and deal with it immediately. If there is any issue that is a bone of contention between yourself and your partner, your best response is to talk about it and find a compromise. Avoid leaving anything to fester today, because the sooner you sort things out, the more happiness you can find later.

30 TUESDAY
Moon Age Day 15   Moon Sign Libra

am . . . .

pm . . . .
Travel and intellectual interests are now positively highlighted, offering you every encouragement to ring the changes in very satisfying ways. Although there may be many opportunities to shine out in social settings today, there could also be moments when all you really want is to be quite alone with someone you love.

31 WEDNESDAY
Moon Age Day 16   Moon Sign Libra

am . . . .

pm . . . .
Trends assist you to give your social life a definite boost around the middle of this week, and you also have what it takes to make people notice just how efficient and fair-minded you can be. By all means be sensitive to the sensibilities of those around you, but there is also much to be said for remaining a little self-centred.

1 THURSDAY
Moon Age Day 17   Moon Sign Scorpio

am . . . .

pm . . . .
You needn't be any sort of April Fool today, except if you choose to look like one for the sake of others. Your sense of fun is definitely to the fore, and you can approach life in a light-hearted but still efficient way. This would be a very good time to put your desires to the test as far as your career is concerned. Money matters could be variable.

2 FRIDAY
Moon Age Day 18   Moon Sign Scorpio

am . . . .

pm . . . .
Much of the day can be beneficial to your family life and should offer you scope to get in touch with people you haven't seen for a while. Make the most of meetings that come along like a bolt from the blue, particularly if these involve someone noteworthy. A day on which you can attract a great deal of interest from others.

3 SATURDAY
Moon Age Day 19   Moon Sign Sagittarius

am . . . .

pm . . . .
This can be a very advantageous time for communications and for getting to grips with issues that have teased your mind in the past. You could do worse than to channel this in the direction of solving puzzles and mysteries in any sphere of your life. Be prepared to make having fun with friends your number one priority this weekend.

4 SUNDAY
Moon Age Day 20   Moon Sign Sagittarius

am . . . .

pm . . . .
There are signs that you could be at odds in some social situations today, particularly if you have to mix with certain people you don't much care for. Putting in that extra bit of effort can make all the difference though, and may help you to gain a new friend into the bargain. Speaking of bargains, today would be ideal for a shopping spree!

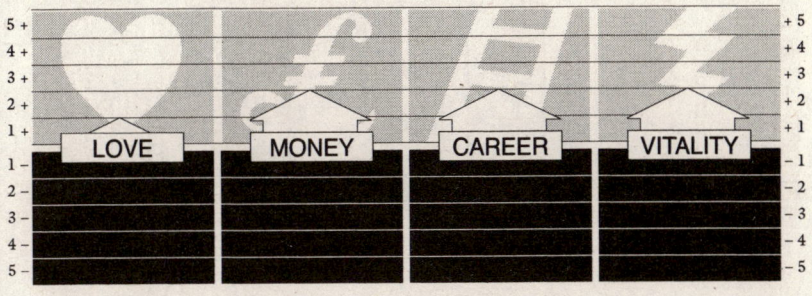

April 2010

YOUR MONTH AT A GLANCE

$\oplus$ = Opportunities are around $\ominus$ = Be on the defensive   ● = Life is pretty ordinary

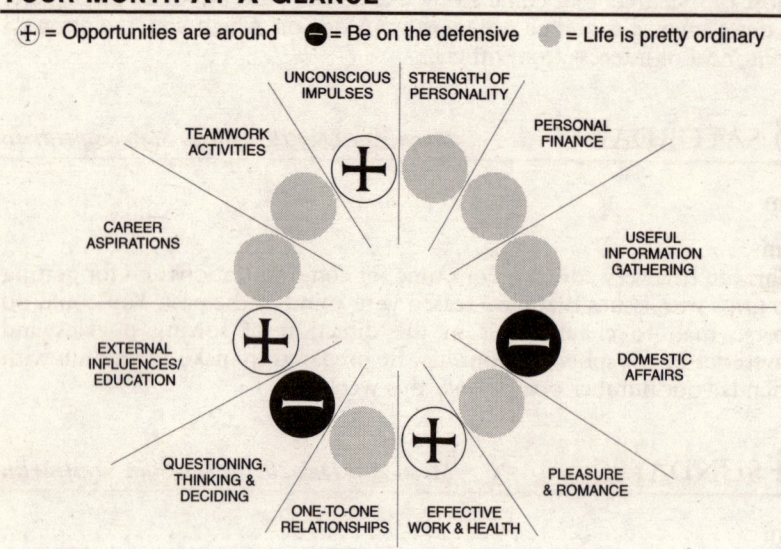

UNCONSCIOUS IMPULSES

STRENGTH OF PERSONALITY

TEAMWORK ACTIVITIES

PERSONAL FINANCE

CAREER ASPIRATIONS

USEFUL INFORMATION GATHERING

EXTERNAL INFLUENCES/ EDUCATION

DOMESTIC AFFAIRS

QUESTIONING, THINKING & DECIDING

PLEASURE & ROMANCE

ONE-TO-ONE RELATIONSHIPS

EFFECTIVE WORK & HEALTH

APRIL HIGHS AND LOWS

Here I show you how the rhythms of the Moon will affect you this month. Like the tide, your energies and abilities will rise and fall with its pattern. When it is above the centre line, go for it, when it is below, you should be resting.

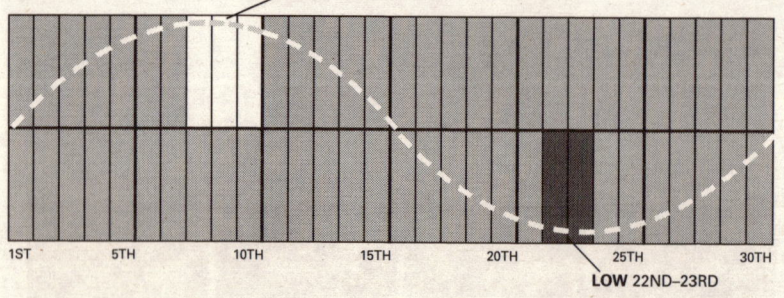

HIGH 8TH–10TH

1ST   5TH   10TH   15TH   20TH   25TH   30TH

LOW 22ND–23RD

5 MONDAY   *Moon Age Day 21   Moon Sign Sagittarius*

am . . . .

pm . . . .
There are opportunities at the moment for heart-to-heart talks, and you can use these to clear the air if there have been any misunderstandings recently. Make sure that you really listen to what people are saying, instead of hearing only what you want to hear. As far as work is concerned, there is much to be said for relying on other people today.

6 TUESDAY   *Moon Age Day 22   Moon Sign Capricorn*

am . . . .

pm . . . .
Significant rewards are there for the taking today, though you may have to turn over a few stones in order to find them. Life can be quite eventful for sons and daughters of Aquarius, but it would also be easy to get bogged down with issues that you can't resolve easily. It pays to keep things light and airy in your associations with others.

7 WEDNESDAY   *Moon Age Day 23   Moon Sign Capricorn*

am . . . .

pm . . . .
You have what it takes to gain the upper hand in talks and debates today, though there may be nothing particularly surprising about that. Bear in mind that not everyone will agree with you, no matter how persuasive you are, and there are some people who will argue more or less on principle. Don't give in to negative thinking regarding new jobs.

8 THURSDAY   *Moon Age Day 24   Moon Sign Aquarius*

am . . . .

pm . . . .
You are in a position to make good progress today, and the lunar high can be very supportive when it comes to monetary matters. Give yourself fully to enjoyment once the responsibilities of the day are out of the way, and arrange for a change of scene if possible. It's all very well being in the mood to party, but will those around you agree?

9 FRIDAY

Moon Age Day 25   Moon Sign Aquarius

am . . . .

pm . . . .

You can be a very positive person at the best of times, but especially so while the lunar high is running the show. Your talent for inspiring other people is always noteworthy but is especially highlighted at the present time. This can be of tremendous use when it comes to getting on at work and seeking any form of advancement.

10 SATURDAY

Moon Age Day 26   Moon Sign Aquarius

am . . . .

pm . . . .

Good luck should still be on your side at the start of the weekend, and you can use your positive frame of mind to get you what you want for at least some of today. You need to be extremely enterprising in your ideas, and what really counts is your ability to get other people on board. Why not plan now for immediate travel or journeys later on?

11 SUNDAY

Moon Age Day 27   Moon Sign Pisces

am . . . .

pm . . . .

A change for the better could well lie in matters to do with hearth and home. Trends assist you to make important contributions to any discussions that are taking place, and to speak honestly and with candour. Don't be too quick to react today if someone seems to be insulting you in some way. Ask yourself whether any offence was intended.

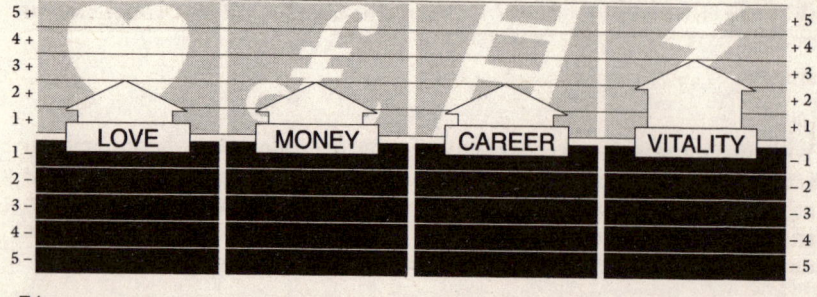

12 MONDAY
Moon Age Day 28   Moon Sign Pisces

am . . . .

pm . . . .
Issues connected to your home life are still under the spotlight, and will offer the best chance of rewards under present planetary trends. Mercury is presently in your solar fourth house and this alone assists you to make your communications with family members both inspiring and extremely useful. Your partner may have a favour to ask.

13 TUESDAY
Moon Age Day 29   Moon Sign Aries

am . . . .

pm . . . .
A day to concentrate your energies on getting new plans off the ground. Quick thinking could save the day more than once this week, and with the Sun in your solar third house you should have little trouble getting others to listen to what you have to say. It's natural to worry about others, particularly young people, but is it necessary just now?

14 WEDNESDAY
Moon Age Day 0   Moon Sign Aries

am . . . .

pm . . . .
Now you should be able to find plenty to keep you interested. Meetings, appointments and discussions are all well accented at the moment. A new exchange of ideas might prove to be rewarding, though it's worth thinking very carefully before you get yourself involved in any activity that will tie you up a great deal.

15 THURSDAY
Moon Age Day 1   Moon Sign Taurus

am . . . .

pm . . . .
You have scope to get a great deal out of your domestic life now and this is linked to the fourth-house planets Mercury and Venus. This would be an ideal day to rest and pamper yourself, or to combine your efforts with those of your partner to forge a new and important path. Whatever you decide to do at this time, starting it at home is the key.

16 FRIDAY

Moon Age Day 2   Moon Sign Taurus

am . . . .

pm . . . .
There are signs of some disputes to sort out in relationships, and you may
have difficulty enjoying the company of people you see as being
overassertive. The trouble is that there can only be one centre of
attention at the moment, and you may subconsciously think that it
should be you. A calm and reasonable approach works best.

17 SATURDAY

Moon Age Day 3   Moon Sign Taurus

am . . . .

pm . . . .
Current influences can do much to assist your social life, though you
could still be crossing swords with anyone who has an ego as big as yours!
On those occasions when you think you are merely sticking up for
yourself, you need to be careful that you are not in fact getting on your
high horse. The more you laugh today, the better.

18 SUNDAY

☿   *Moon Age Day 4   Moon Sign Gemini*

am . . . .

pm . . . .
This can be a relaxing time if you stick around the homestead, and there
are certainly favourable trends around in that area of your life. However,
it might actually be too comfortable, because there are other elements in
your nature at the moment that are urging you to find excitement and
even risk. Try to balance things out sensibly.

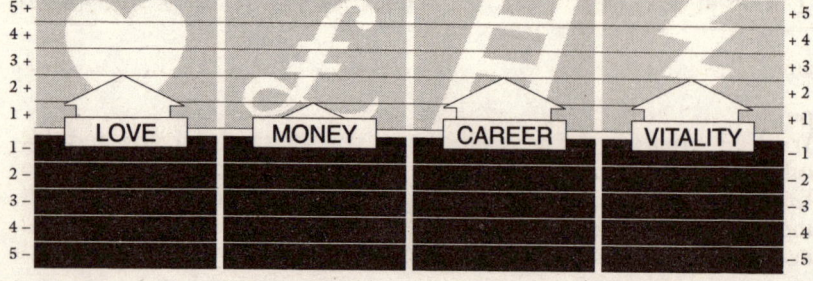

19 MONDAY ☿ *Moon Age Day 5 Moon Sign Gemini*

am . . . .

pm . . . .
Co-operation is the name of the game at work, and your strength lies in your willingness to take on new responsibilities, even if some of these are a little scary at first. Be prepared to respond if others want to rely on you and to trust your judgement. You also have an opportunity to improve your love life at present.

20 TUESDAY ☿ *Moon Age Day 6 Moon Sign Cancer*

am . . . .

pm . . . .
For now the Sun remains in your solar third house and this could turn out to be especially favourable for entertaining and for thinking up new ideas. In a couple of days the Sun moves on, so make the most of the opportunities it presents just now. There are gains to be made on the financial front, though you may have to search for them.

21 WEDNESDAY ☿ *Moon Age Day 7 Moon Sign Cancer*

am . . . .

pm . . . .
There's nothing wrong with changing your professional plans if you want to spend more time sorting out domestic issues and personal wishes. Even if you are fulfilling your responsibilities well enough, it might be difficult to show quite your usual level of responsibility at work. A change of scenery could work wonders at any time today.

22 THURSDAY ☿ *Moon Age Day 8 Moon Sign Leo*

am . . . .

pm . . . .
With the lunar low arriving you might be less inclined to push yourself or to put yourself forward in company. For the moment there is much to be said for being an 'also ran', even if this is usually quite contrary to your nature. Despite the potentially quiet interlude, it's still important to be available if others need to make contact with you.

23 FRIDAY ☿ *Moon Age Day 9   Moon Sign Leo*

am . . . .

pm . . . .
Keep a low profile, get on with something fairly simple and hum a little song. That's the best way to deal with the lunar low. When you are not doing practical things you might decide to read a good book or magazine and to put your feet up for once. You can afford to let family pressures flow over you – or let someone else sort them out!

24 SATURDAY ☿ *Moon Age Day 10   Moon Sign Virgo*

am . . . .

pm . . . .
There are so many fourth-house influences in your chart at this time that remaining committed to your domestic circumstances counts for a great deal. Be prepared to spend any spare time you have this weekend with relatives, and to focus your efforts on bringing both order and happiness to your abode.

25 SUNDAY ☿ *Moon Age Day 11   Moon Sign Virgo*

am . . . .

pm . . . .
The time is right to follow your feelings regarding a personal issue. Family matters continue to be the main source of any rewards that you can achieve, and you might have good reason to be proud of younger family members or your partner today. Beware of taking on a massive workload, and find time today to move around freely.

	LOVE	MONEY	CAREER	VITALITY	
5 +					+ 5
4 +					+ 4
3 +					+ 3
2 +					+ 2
1 +					+ 1
1 –					– 1
2 –					– 2
3 –					– 3
4 –					– 4
5 –					– 5

26 MONDAY ☿ *Moon Age Day 12   Moon Sign Libra*

am . . . .

pm . . . .
The planetary emphasis is now quite clearly on your love life. Venus has moved out of your fourth house and into the fifth. You should also be taking advantage of greater freedom to do what pleases you. Trends allow you to cut back on the significant sense of responsibility for loved ones that has been around for a few weeks.

27 TUESDAY ☿ *Moon Age Day 13   Moon Sign Libra*

am . . . .

pm . . . .
The present position of Mars indicates that total harmony in personal attachments is probably something you cannot rely upon today – at least not without putting in a little effort. What really counts is avoiding getting annoyed if people snap at you. Ask yourself whether their attitude is inspired by you, and be prepared to take it in your stride.

28 WEDNESDAY ☿ *Moon Age Day 14   Moon Sign Scorpio*

am . . . .

pm . . . .
There needn't be a dull moment at home right now, and with little Mercury still there in your solar fourth house you have what it takes to make sure that conversations with family members are inspiring and fun. If you sense the time is right for a deep family discussion, there are good reasons to get it out of the way today.

29 THURSDAY ☿ *Moon Age Day 15   Moon Sign Scorpio*

am . . . .

pm . . . .
This could be one of your better days for making preparations or for getting out into the fresh air. The busiest Aquarians may not have even noticed that spring is painting the hedgerows, but there is much to be said for making sure you register the fact. You will soon be able to capitalise on a more dynamic phase, but for now you can afford to relax.

30 FRIDAY ☿ *Moon Age Day 16   Moon Sign Scorpio*

am . . . .

pm . . . .
Social matters can offer you scope for real pleasure, and starting the
weekend early would be no bad thing. News you gain from far off can be
enlivening and even fascinating, and contact with relatives or friends who
live in other parts of the world can make all the difference now. Be
sensible regarding purchases around this time.

1 SATURDAY ☿ *Moon Age Day 17   Moon Sign Sagittarius*

am . . . .

pm . . . .
Venus assists you to give your love life a real boost, and this has potential
to be a really fascinating sort of weekend as far as personal attachments
are concerned. The time is right to reach a much better understanding
with your lover and to find new facets to your intimate relationships that
will pep things up. A day for sharing secrets.

2 SUNDAY ☿ *Moon Age Day 18   Moon Sign Sagittarius*

am . . . .

pm . . . .
You would be wise to focus on your health today. The Moon is not in a
particularly positive position for you, bringing the possibility of minor
problems or even silly mishaps. This would not be the best time to take
undue risks and you need to stop and think before putting yourself in
harm's way. Be prepared to respond if friends seek you out.

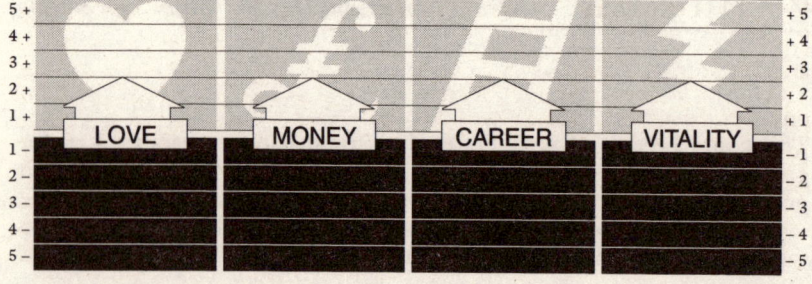

May 2010

YOUR MONTH AT A GLANCE

⊕ = Opportunities are around   ⊖ = Be on the defensive   ● = Life is pretty ordinary

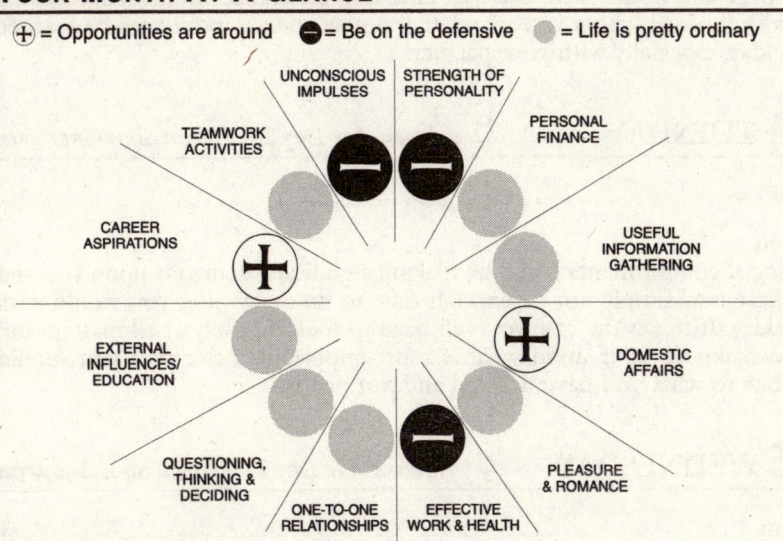

UNCONSCIOUS IMPULSES

STRENGTH OF PERSONALITY

TEAMWORK ACTIVITIES

PERSONAL FINANCE

CAREER ASPIRATIONS

USEFUL INFORMATION GATHERING

EXTERNAL INFLUENCES/ EDUCATION

DOMESTIC AFFAIRS

QUESTIONING, THINKING & DECIDING

PLEASURE & ROMANCE

ONE-TO-ONE RELATIONSHIPS

EFFECTIVE WORK & HEALTH

MAY HIGHS AND LOWS

Here I show you how the rhythms of the Moon will affect you this month. Like the tide, your energies and abilities will rise and fall with its pattern. When it is above the centre line, go for it, when it is below, you should be resting.

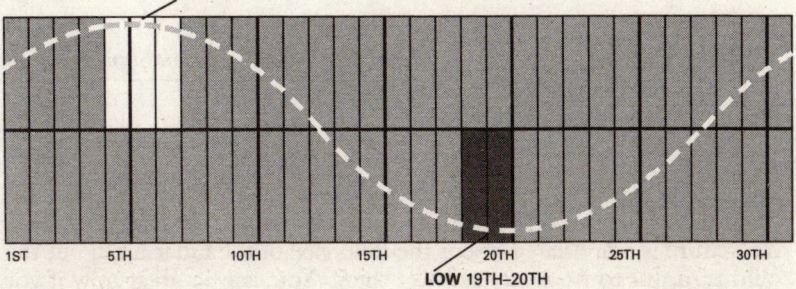

HIGH 5TH–7TH

1ST   5TH   10TH   15TH   20TH   25TH   30TH

LOW 19TH–20TH

3 MONDAY   ☿   *Moon Age Day 19   Moon Sign Capricorn*

am . . . .

pm . . . .
Little Mercury is almost stationary in the heavens at present, at least it is
as far as you are concerned. This keeps the emphasis firmly placed on
house and home, with the best talks and general communications being
with those to whom you are related. A new understanding can be reached
today, especially with your partner.

4 TUESDAY   ☿   *Moon Age Day 20   Moon Sign Capricorn*

am . . . .

pm . . . .
Social commitments could be making significant demands upon you and
there may simply not be enough time to do everything you would wish
today. If this is the case you will need to look carefully at all matters and
to make up your mind what is most important. After that you should
stick to what you have decided and not deviate.

5 WEDNESDAY   ☿   *Moon Age Day 21   Moon Sign Aquarius*

am . . . .

pm . . . .
Along comes the lunar high and with it the chance to tap into better luck
and more instant gratification. In any areas of your life that have been
static or tedious recently, you now have scope to inject some fun and
enthusiasm. Almost anything you decide to do at the moment is well
accented, even when you know you are taking risks.

6 THURSDAY   ☿   *Moon Age Day 22   Moon Sign Aquarius*

am . . . .

pm . . . .
Someone might be more than willing to do you a great favour today, and
you probably won't do yourself any harm by asking. The cheekier side of
your nature is emphasised under the influence of the lunar high, but this
could turn out to be a very positive thing. You can be great now if you
make full use of your sense of fun.

7 FRIDAY ☿ *Moon Age Day 23 Moon Sign Aquarius*

am ....

pm ....

The reactions you can attract from loved ones should now be very positive, and you give of your best when mixing with those who adore you. Unfortunately this cannot be everyone, even if you think it should be. There are certain lost causes in terms of people you know, and you would be wise to accept the fact.

8 SATURDAY ☿ *Moon Age Day 24 Moon Sign Pisces*

am ....

pm ....

You can afford to let the needs of the world fade into the background this weekend as you turn your full attention, once again, to your home. The Sun is in your solar fourth house, making this an ideal time to improve things on the domestic scene, perhaps in a material way. Physical activity is well starred for you under present planetary trends.

9 SUNDAY ☿ *Moon Age Day 25 Moon Sign Pisces*

am ....

pm ....

You could now be challenged to overcome selfish tendencies and to show just how charitable and giving you are capable of being. For perhaps the first time this year the really quirky side of Aquarius is also highlighted. Could people describe you as being slightly eccentric? Be prepared to laugh at labels of this sort.

	LOVE	MONEY	CAREER	VITALITY
5 +				+ 5
4 +				+ 4
3 +				+ 3
2 +				+ 2
1 +				+ 1
1 −				− 1
2 −				− 2
3 −				− 3
4 −				− 4
5 −				− 5

10 MONDAY ☿ *Moon Age Day 26   Moon Sign Aries*

am . . . .

pm . . . .
The time is right to exhibit all your charisma and to show yourself to the
world in the best light. In social settings it's possible for you to play the
fool, and your personality should be extremely attractive to those around
you. This is one of the most favourable times to be an Aquarian,
particularly if you make the most of your unique nature.

11 TUESDAY ☿ *Moon Age Day 27   Moon Sign Aries*

am . . . .

pm . . . .
It's time to try out some new ideas and to be bold and enterprising in
almost everything you do. Why not get involved in discussions and show
those you are talking to just how deep and wide your intelligence actually
is? You can learn much about the world today by simply keeping your
eyes and ears open.

12 WEDNESDAY ☿ *Moon Age Day 28   Moon Sign Aries*

am . . . .

pm . . . .
There is much to be said for slackening professional progress for a day or
two. Whilst the Moon is in your solar fourth house you are encouraged
to spend your time thinking about home-based matters rather than those
out in the wider world, but from a social point of view you can still be
number one. Finances might need attention now.

13 THURSDAY *Moon Age Day 29   Moon Sign Taurus*

am . . . .

pm . . . .
Trends now place a strong emphasis on personal and family concerns.
Outside obligations are best put on hold for a while to give you a chance
to respond to those fourth-house planets. Be prepared to deal with
demands that come in and to capitalise quickly on situations that you
know instinctively could work for you in the future.

14 FRIDAY
Moon Age Day 0   Moon Sign Taurus

am . . . .

pm . . . .
With relationships now having potential for a little more sparkle, spending time with people you feel close to is the order of the day. It pays to start the weekend early and make Friday night special for yourself and for those closest to you. This would be an ideal opportunity to introduce any topics of conversation that were previously taboo.

15 SATURDAY
Moon Age Day 1   Moon Sign Gemini

am . . . .

pm . . . .
The planetary influences around you at this time could stir up restless feelings, and the need for fun and romance is paramount. This can be easily fulfilled, as can your desire to widen your immediate friendship circle. There ought to be plenty of energy available, and you might even decide to channel it into some new and boisterous pastime.

16 SUNDAY
Moon Age Day 2   Moon Sign Gemini

am . . . .

pm . . . .
Ask yourself whether long-term relationships are at the root of problems you encounter today. Maybe people don't understand what you have been trying to say to them and are reacting sharply as a result. Your best response is to explain yourself again, slowly and considerately. Family members could well prove intransigent now.

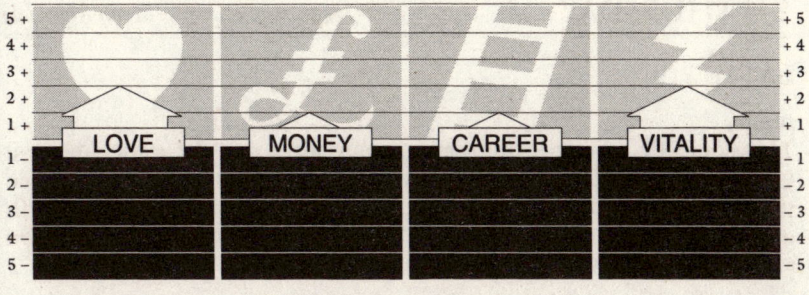

17 MONDAY
Moon Age Day 3   Moon Sign Cancer

am . . . .

pm . . . .
This is not the best time to change your mind regarding practical matters, though you do have scope to reorganise things in your working life. This is a favourable period for communications of all sorts, particularly those that make use of state-of-the-art technology. New skills can be learned very easily under present planetary trends.

18 TUESDAY
Moon Age Day 4   Moon Sign Cancer

am . . . .

pm . . . .
Leisure and pleasure pursuits have potential to be your most rewarding area around now. You can afford to be dynamic and very expressive, which assists you to influence and impress some fairly important people. Not everyone will be on your wavelength, and you need to remember that you can't be universally popular and unique.

19 WEDNESDAY
Moon Age Day 5   Moon Sign Leo

am . . . .

pm . . . .
Life might seem somewhat dreary today but it really depends on the way you approach the lunar low. If you keep an open mind and refuse to get down in the dumps about things that are not of any real importance, you may barely notice this planetary visit. Try different responses to the same old potential problems.

20 THURSDAY
Moon Age Day 6   Moon Sign Leo

am . . . .

pm . . . .
This could be a fairly taxing day in some ways, but the same advice as yesterday still holds good. Pretend you are feeling extremely positive and use your imagination to solve any immediate concerns you have. With ingenuity and enterprise you can turn rain clouds inside out. You can create an especially heart-warming interlude this evening.

21 FRIDAY
Moon Age Day 7   Moon Sign Virgo

am . . . .

pm . . . .
Anything to do with your career or practical matters is particularly well
accented at this time. It's all about your great sense of purpose and your
desire to get onside with people you recognise as being life's winners.
Shining out like a star, you can fill a room with your charisma, and this
helps you to make plenty of friends on your journey.

22 SATURDAY
Moon Age Day 8   Moon Sign Virgo

am . . . .

pm . . . .
Brand new romantic developments are favoured and planetary trends
generally assist you to be in the right place to benefit from personal
attachments. Finding the right words to let someone know how you feel
isn't usually difficult for you, but at the moment it's a piece of cake. An
ideal time to get together with people you don't see too often.

23 SUNDAY
Moon Age Day 9   Moon Sign Virgo

am . . . .

pm . . . .
It's worth keeping self-righteous behaviour at bay and not thinking or
pretending you have all the answers. If you are willing to ask for advice
people should be prepared to help you out. Standard responses to the
enquiries of family members might not be enough to satisfy them, and
you may need to be quite ingenious.

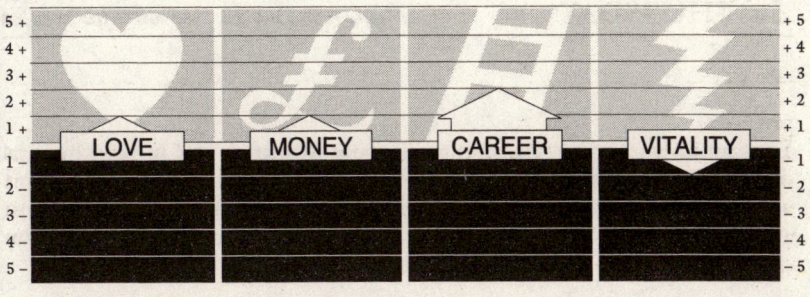

24 MONDAY
Moon Age Day 10   Moon Sign Libra

am . . . .

pm . . . .
It pays to do what you can to enlarge your social circle this week. The more people you know, the greater is the chance that you can gain their support when it matters the most. A new and interesting period is on offer now that the Sun is entering your solar fifth house, and it allows you scope to get away at last from some of the domestic issues.

25 TUESDAY
Moon Age Day 11   Moon Sign Libra

am . . . .

pm . . . .
Venus is moving rapidly through your chart and from its present position it can be very helpful as far as your work is concerned. It should now be possible to mix business with pleasure and to extend your impact to people you haven't previously influenced. Trends also support an emotional and nostalgic interlude at the moment.

26 WEDNESDAY
Moon Age Day 12   Moon Sign Scorpio

am . . . .

pm . . . .
There are forces at work that can assist you to get what you want right now, especially where practical matters are concerned. You are in a position to sort out jobs that usually take an age in a fraction of the normal time and to get everything to fall into place. If this leaves you with time on your hands, why not use it socially?

27 THURSDAY
Moon Age Day 13   Moon Sign Scorpio

am . . . .

pm . . . .
You can now afford to be highly outgoing in speech and in your general manner. This helps you to get people to notice you and to appreciate how well you are working. You usually have something funny to say, but just at present you can demonstrate the resourcefulness and wit of a stand-up comedian. Friends matter greatly now.

28 FRIDAY
Moon Age Day 14   Moon Sign Sagittarius

am . . . .

pm . . . .
Today offers a high spot on the domestic scene but probably less aggravation and worry at home than might have been the case recently. If you manage to create enjoyment and contentment close to home, there is less compulsion to move around much today or across the weekend. By all means invite friends round and socialise!

29 SATURDAY
Moon Age Day 15   Moon Sign Sagittarius

am . . . .

pm . . . .
You now tend to thrive in situations that allow you to throw in your lot with others. Aquarius is usually willing to co-operate, but the results of doing so now are much greater than you might imagine. New hobbies or pastimes are well marked, and trends encourage you to find something quite ingenious and novel to fill part of this weekend.

30 SUNDAY
Moon Age Day 16   Moon Sign Capricorn

am . . . .

pm . . . .
It might be beneficial today if you could find a few moments to be totally alone. The Moon has moved into your solar twelfth house, supporting a slightly more reserved interlude in which it's worth thinking things through on your own. This doesn't mean you have to isolate yourself in any way, but a little contemplation can make all the difference.

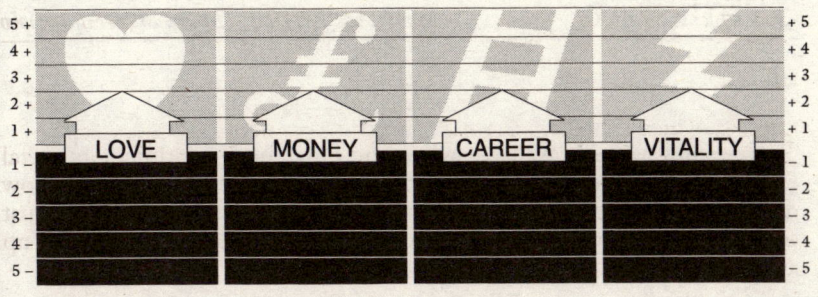

31 MONDAY
Moon Age Day 17   Moon Sign Capricorn

am . . . .

pm . . . .
Make the most of opportunities for personal and romantic moments today, even if these are when you least expect them. This is linked to the planet Venus, which is in a favourable position to assist your love life to flourish and bloom. Just as the flowers presently grow all around, it's time to let your romantic world open up to the summer.

1 TUESDAY
Moon Age Day 18   Moon Sign Capricorn

am . . . .

pm . . . .
On the first day of June you can afford to feel optimistic, though a little reserve would be no bad thing. The time is right to finish off any tasks that have been getting on your nerves and to look at old matters in a completely different light. Rather than taking any decisive action, you would be wise to bide your soul in patience until tomorrow.

2 WEDNESDAY
Moon Age Day 19   Moon Sign Aquarius

am . . . .

pm . . . .
An expanded self-confidence enables you to speak out, even if you are not too sure what you should be saying. The lunar high encourages you to act on impulse and to do what you know is right. It's important to keep your communication charming yet forceful. Is anyone willing to counter your arguments now?

3 THURSDAY
Moon Age Day 20   Moon Sign Aquarius

am . . . .

pm . . . .
There is always luck available when the lunar high is around, but the effect is even stronger this month. What matters the most is how delightful you are to know, and great happiness is possible if you can get others to make a real fuss of you. Certain benefits can be gained today as a result of your past efforts.

4 FRIDAY

Moon Age Day 21   Moon Sign Pisces

am ....

pm ....
With the Sun in its present position new creative and romantic pursuits are there for the taking. You should know what you want from life, even if you are not always sure how to get it. Be prepared to ask some leading questions and listen carefully to the answers. You might be surprised at the actions of someone you thought you knew.

5 SATURDAY

Moon Age Day 22   Moon Sign Pisces

am ....

pm ....
Newer and better chances are on offer in terms of your financial planning, and you have what it takes to make gains at every turn. It's natural for friendships to have ups and downs, and this may be no fault of yours. The time is probably right to seek new attachments, perhaps even people you used to know in the dim and distant past.

6 SUNDAY

Moon Age Day 23   Moon Sign Pisces

am ....

pm ....
The spotlight is on your ability to make all the right moves when it comes to being noticed. Life does you a few favours without you having to do anything to inspire them, and you can capitalise on good luck that follows you around like a shadow for a few days. A favourable time for your love life and for showing your romantic side.

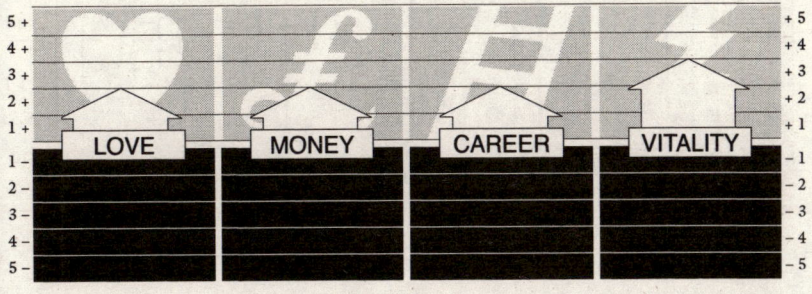

June 2010

YOUR MONTH AT A GLANCE

⊕ = Opportunities are around   ⊖ = Be on the defensive   ● = Life is pretty ordinary

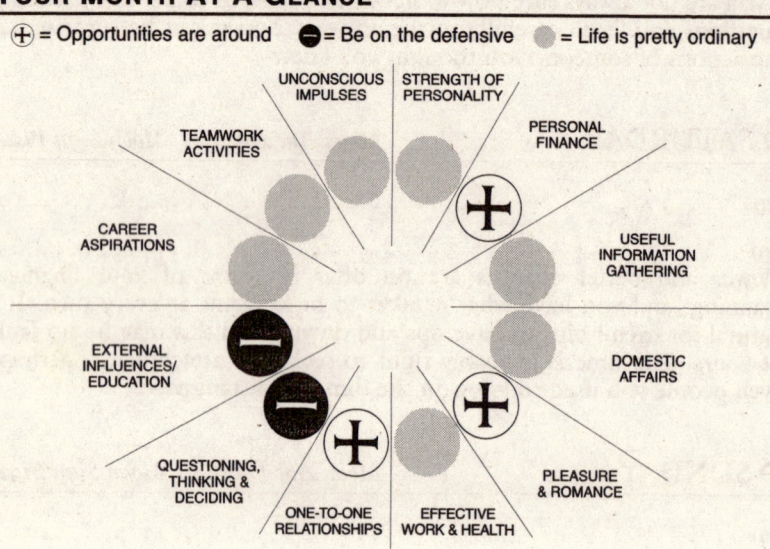

UNCONSCIOUS IMPULSES

STRENGTH OF PERSONALITY

PERSONAL FINANCE

TEAMWORK ACTIVITIES

CAREER ASPIRATIONS

USEFUL INFORMATION GATHERING

EXTERNAL INFLUENCES/ EDUCATION

DOMESTIC AFFAIRS

QUESTIONING, THINKING & DECIDING

PLEASURE & ROMANCE

ONE-TO-ONE RELATIONSHIPS

EFFECTIVE WORK & HEALTH

JUNE HIGHS AND LOWS

Here I show you how the rhythms of the Moon will affect you this month. Like the tide, your energies and abilities will rise and fall with its pattern. When it is above the centre line, go for it, when it is below, you should be resting. **HIGH 2ND–3RD**

HIGH 29TH–30TH

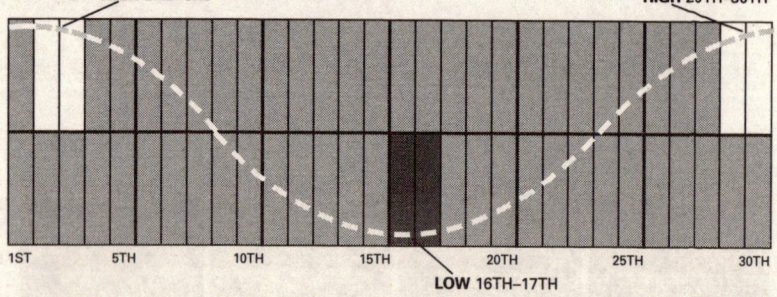

1ST   5TH   10TH   15TH   20TH   25TH   30TH

LOW 16TH–17TH

7 MONDAY
Moon Age Day 24 Moon Sign Aries

am . . . .

pm . . . .
This is a period during which you have scope to make progress with less effort than might usually be the case. You should also have things to smile about as far as your career is concerned, and you are in a position to turn heads in a positive way wherever you go. This is Aquarius showing itself at its very best.

8 TUESDAY
Moon Age Day 25 Moon Sign Aries

am . . . .

pm . . . .
You can now boost your mood and general peace of mind through your nearest and dearest and the way they are behaving at home. Mercury remains in your solar fourth house for the moment, so communications with people on the domestic scene remain favoured. You can use this influence to bury old hatchets and reach new understandings.

9 WEDNESDAY
Moon Age Day 26 Moon Sign Taurus

am . . . .

pm . . . .
Any sort of high-profile situation would suit you today and you can get more or less what you want by using the force of your personality. Being generous to others is fine, though bear in mind that you might not always be getting the best from them. You needn't worry too much as long as you have control over your own destiny in the main.

10 THURSDAY
Moon Age Day 27 Moon Sign Taurus

am . . . .

pm . . . .
This may not be the most stable part of the year as far as your personal life is concerned. Even if nothing major is going wrong, little niggles and seemingly pointless irritations are a distinct possibility. Your best response is to turn your attention outwards to the wider world and the people on the periphery of your life.

11 FRIDAY   *Moon Age Day 28   Moon Sign Gemini*

am . . . .

pm . . . .
Trends assist you to score successes at work and to make a good
impression when it counts. If not everyone is keen to follow your lead, it
pays to concentrate on those who are, rather than wasting time on lost
causes. In terms of finances, you need to look carefully at investments and
avoid making significant commitments for the next few days.

12 SATURDAY   *Moon Age Day 0   Moon Sign Gemini*

am . . . .

pm . . . .
Make sure that nobody tops you in the personality stakes at the moment!
Mercury has moved on at last and now occupies your solar fifth house.
Success is available for many of your actions, and it's worth having an
'immediate' response to situations as they unfold around you. In most
respects you should be on top form now.

13 SUNDAY   *Moon Age Day 1   Moon Sign Gemini*

am . . . .

pm . . . .
This is an auspicious period for developing your practical strengths,
especially at work. Of course this might not be possible on a Sunday, but
if you also have your planning head on you should be able to sort things
out in your mind ahead of a new push later. You can also afford to think
about travelling, either now or very soon.

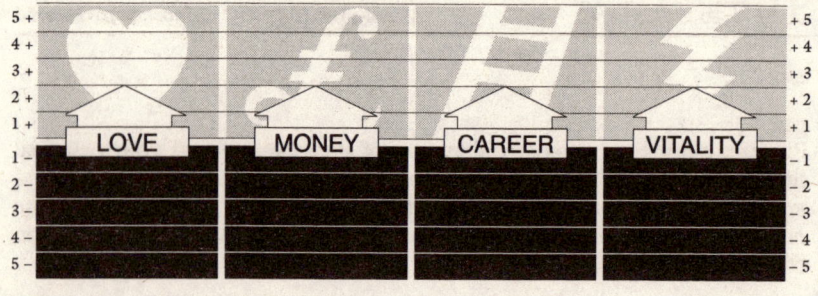

14 MONDAY

Moon Age Day 2   Moon Sign Cancer

am . . . .

pm . . . .
Most of the time you are in a position to feel fairly positive about both professional and personal matters. You have an opportunity to make a favourable impression on others and to make some fairly important new friends around now. Remember that there could be people quite close to you now who might help where your ambitions are concerned.

15 TUESDAY

Moon Age Day 3   Moon Sign Cancer

am . . . .

pm . . . .
Comfort and security could definitely be on your agenda, though not in a particularly significant way, and you should still be willing to take the odd risk, at least for today. You might decide that the way you approach others needs some modification, especially if someone is not responding in the way you would normally expect.

16 WEDNESDAY

Moon Age Day 4   Moon Sign Leo

am . . . .

pm . . . .
This is a time for rest and reflection because the more you try to move forward at a pace, the stickier things could seem. The lunar low needn't make you depressed, because after all it only lasts for a couple of days. Your best response is to keep a sense of proportion and don't get carried away with pointless or imaginary worries.

17 THURSDAY

Moon Age Day 5   Moon Sign Leo

am . . . .

pm . . . .
Positive influences now attend your love life, though you might decide that making any sort of practical progress is impossible. There is much to be said for opting for the simple and for not making waves in relationships. This is the best time of the month to stand and watch things happen rather than getting yourself too involved.

18 FRIDAY
Moon Age Day 6   Moon Sign Virgo

am . . . .

pm . . . .
If some of the strategies for success that you have been using of late have
outlived their usefulness, the time is now right for a reappraisal. Mars is
in your solar eighth house and this encourages you to look again and to
take quite significant action where necessary. A slightly more blunt
approach than usual is indicated, so be careful what you say.

19 SATURDAY
Moon Age Day 7   Moon Sign Virgo

am . . . .

pm . . . .
Your natural leadership abilities, including your personal power and
charm, are all strongly emphasised around now. Ensure that you focus on
essentials today because you have a great ability to get what you want but
you could 'wander' a little in your planning. Make the most of the chance
to improve your social life.

20 SUNDAY
Moon Age Day 8   Moon Sign Libra

am . . . .

pm . . . .
There isn't much doubt about your creative drive, or your present ability
to get things right first time. Will your usual routines be sufficiently
fulfilling? There are certainly good reasons to seek out change and
diversity in order to avoid becoming bored. If you don't ring the
changes, restlessness could well be the result.

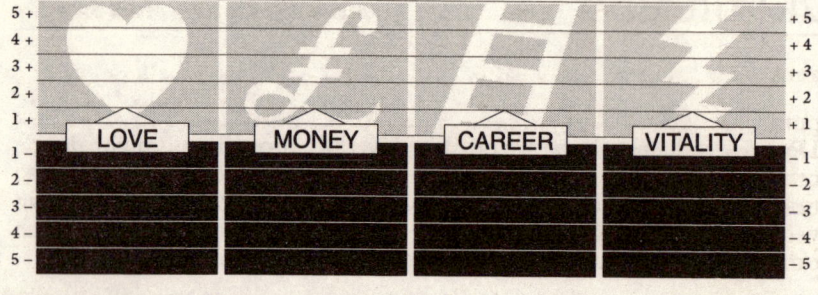

21 MONDAY

Moon Age Day 9   Moon Sign Libra

am . . . .

pm . . . .
Look towards a change of scenery and a diversification of your talents whenever it proves to be possible this week. There are gains to be made on the financial front, though you shouldn't rely on good luck for these, but rather on your own efforts. An ideal time to allow people from the past to figure significantly in your life again.

22 TUESDAY

Moon Age Day 10   Moon Sign Scorpio

am . . . .

pm . . . .
If you make full use of your talent for delegating work, it shouldn't be difficult at the moment for you to get other people to follow your instructions. Trends suggest that you might spend more of your time supervising others, both at work and at home, than actually getting stuck in yourself. There is also a focus on the way you look.

23 WEDNESDAY

Moon Age Day 11   Moon Sign Scorpio

am . . . .

pm . . . .
You have scope to make this one of the best days of the month in a professional sense, particularly if you can get things to fall into line quite easily. In a personal sense the spotlight is on your great appeal and your ability to turn heads more or less wherever you go. This can be very gratifying, but also embarrassing on occasions!

24 THURSDAY

Moon Age Day 12   Moon Sign Sagittarius

am . . . .

pm . . . .
Dealings with others have potential to be pleasant and rewarding, and so can assist you to feel fairly satisfied with your lot in life. Much of this has to do with the charm you exude in a whole range of situations and your willingness to keep a smile on your face. Your ability to relate to others is one of the skills of the Aquarian.

25 FRIDAY
Moon Age Day 13   Moon Sign Sagittariu

am . . . .

pm . . . .
Capitalise on new opportunities that come your way and explore new methods of getting ahead in both a personal and a professional way. Your ability to mix business with pleasure is especially well marked under present planetary trends. Look for chances to open up new social avenues, particularly later in the day.

26 SATURDAY
Moon Age Day 14   Moon Sign Sagittarius

am . . . .

pm . . . .
There shouldn't be much doubt about your 'wow' factor this weekend, and if you want to make a good impression on one particular individual, now would be a favourable time to go for it. There is much to be said for starting new relationships at this time, or for strengthening existing ties and adding a touch of fun.

27 SUNDAY
Moon Age Day 15   Moon Sign Capricorn

am . . . .

pm . . . .
You have what it takes to create some happy social situations and to make the most of what a summer Sunday has to offer. Under present trends you may not want to be held back or kept in the same place for long. The Air-sign qualities of Aquarius are now to the fore, and these demand that you mix and mingle just as much as possible.

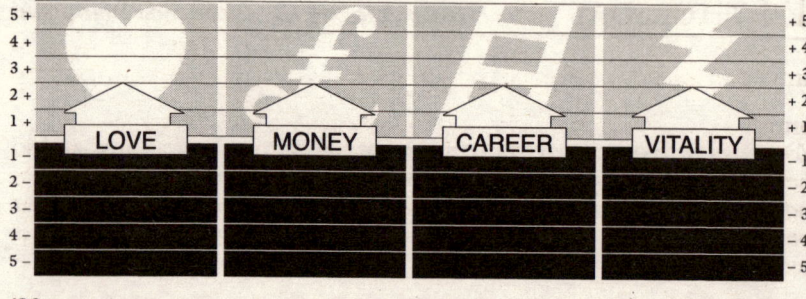

28 MONDAY
Moon Age Day 16   Moon Sign Capricorn

am . . . .

pm . . . .
It's worth finding moments today to mull over your present progress and to plan for your next moves, especially in your professional life. From a social point of view you should be willing to dump anything that is no longer working for you and look towards new possibilities that are on the horizon. Be prepared to support friends.

29 TUESDAY
Moon Age Day 17   Moon Sign Aquarius

am . . . .

pm . . . .
Hooray! The Moon is now back in your sign and brings with it one of the most potent lunar highs you are likely to experience this year. With the Sun in its present position you should be raring to go and enjoying everything that life has to offer. It's a fact of life that if people can't keep up with your pace at the moment, they will be left behind.

30 WEDNESDAY
Moon Age Day 18   Moon Sign Aquarius

am . . . .

pm . . . .
There is good scope for personal gain right now, perhaps even in terms of more money coming in. This may be as much about how you make use of good luck as about sensible planning, though you can be quite ingenious too. If you want to shine when you are in the public eye, you couldn't pick a better time to do so than right now.

1 THURSDAY
Moon Age Day 19   Moon Sign Aquarius

am . . . .

pm . . . .
You need to concentrate today on whatever field you understand the best. This is not because you fail to show an interest in life across the board, merely that you are presently at your most potent. In a professional sense it might feel as if you cannot put a foot wrong. You just seem to have 'it' – whatever it might be!

2 FRIDAY
Moon Age Day 20   Moon Sign Pisc

am . . . .

pm . . . .
Now you need to be reaching out both socially and geographically. Th
world is a very small place these days and communicating regularly wit
people on other continents is not unusual. The more you are able t
spread your philosophy on life, the better you can persuade people t
understand you and respond in a positive way.

3 SATURDAY
Moon Age Day 21   Moon Sign Pisc

am . . . .

pm . . . .
You can deal with many and varied issues whilst the planets occupy thei
present positions. There isn't much doubt now about your Aquaria
credentials and your ability to display yourself at your very best, especiall
in the way you look. It pays to keep abreast of local news and get involve
in things that are going on in your vicinity.

4 SUNDAY
Moon Age Day 22   Moon Sign Arie

am . . . .

pm . . . .
This is a time of fresh opportunities and new ideas. Some of th
restrictions that dogged you earlier in the year are now completely out o
the way, allowing you to be quite certain of the path you are takin
through life. Is everyone around you equally sure about their own life
Be prepared to offer some counselling.

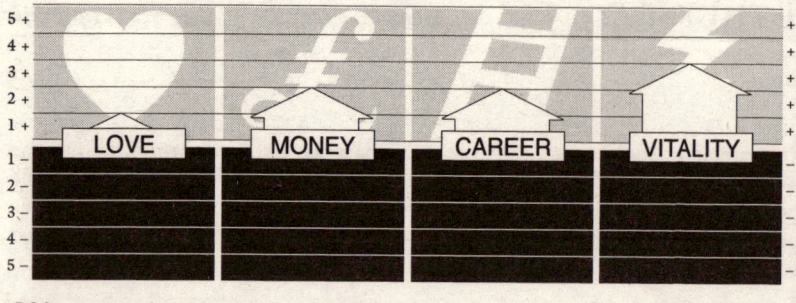

July 2010

YOUR MONTH AT A GLANCE

⊕ = Opportunities are around   ⊖ = Be on the defensive   ⬤ = Life is pretty ordinary

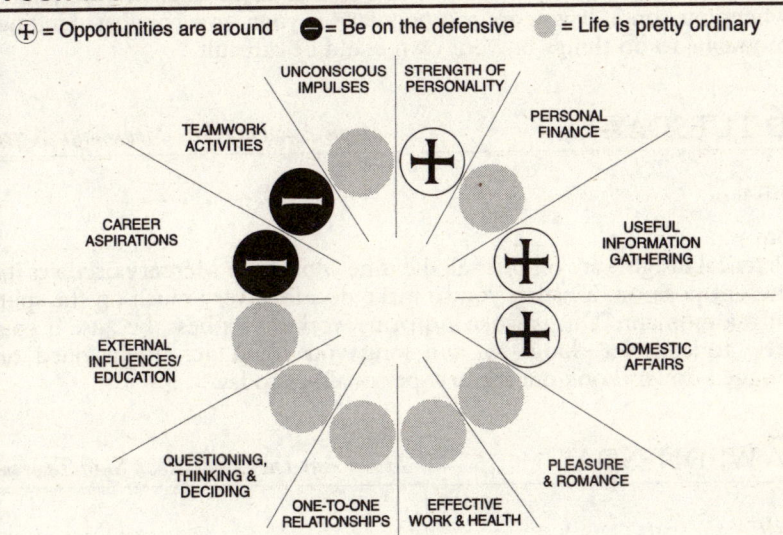

- UNCONSCIOUS IMPULSES
- STRENGTH OF PERSONALITY
- PERSONAL FINANCE
- TEAMWORK ACTIVITIES
- CAREER ASPIRATIONS
- USEFUL INFORMATION GATHERING
- EXTERNAL INFLUENCES/EDUCATION
- DOMESTIC AFFAIRS
- QUESTIONING, THINKING & DECIDING
- PLEASURE & ROMANCE
- ONE-TO-ONE RELATIONSHIPS
- EFFECTIVE WORK & HEALTH

JULY HIGHS AND LOWS

Here I show you how the rhythms of the Moon will affect you this month. Like the tide, your energies and abilities will rise and fall with its pattern. When it is above the centre line, go for it, when it is below, you should be resting. **HIGH** 1ST   **HIGH** 26TH–28TH

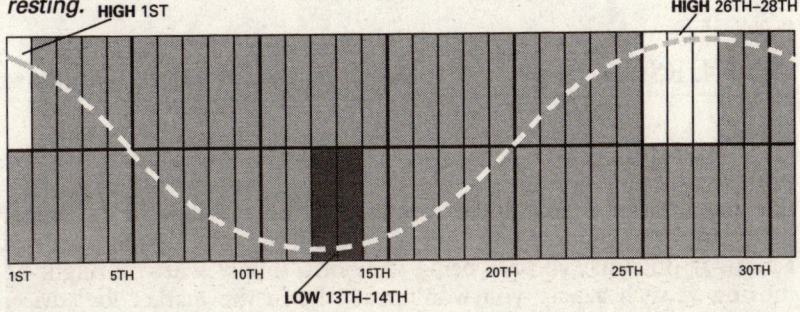

1ST   5TH   10TH   15TH   20TH   25TH   30TH

LOW 13TH–14TH

5 MONDAY
Moon Age Day 23   Moon Sign Aries

am . . . .

pm . . . .
The spotlight now turns towards partnerships, especially those that have a romantic dimension. It shouldn't be hard for you to make friends and influence people at the moment, and in fact there might be occasions when you consider you are too popular for your own comfort. Finding moments to do things on your own could be difficult.

6 TUESDAY
Moon Age Day 24   Moon Sign Aries

am . . . .

pm . . . .
Practical insights are on offer all the time while little Mercury occupies its present position, assisting you to make decisions very much on the spur of the moment. This is when Aquarius works at its best, because if you stop to consider things for too long you could get disillusioned or bogged down. Look out for new personalities today.

7 WEDNESDAY
Moon Age Day 25   Moon Sign Taurus

am . . . .

pm . . . .
New factors arise today, and some of these offer you a chance to think again about issues you thought you understood only too well. It is really a question of integrating new insights into your present and future plans, because your intuition counts for a great deal now. Don't be surprised if some people don't want to co-operate today.

8 THURSDAY
Moon Age Day 26   Moon Sign Taurus

am . . . .

pm . . . .
For much of the time today you have what it takes to be highly industrious and shouldn't be easily diverted from your chosen course of action. It isn't that you are being stubborn, simply that you might be moving at such a pace you won't really be in the market for advice. Socially speaking, do you need to slow things down a little?

9 FRIDAY

Moon Age Day 27   Moon Sign Gemini

am . . . .

pm . . . .
Having a good eye for detail is fine, and it's natural to be upset if things are not the way you think they should be. However, other people have a point of view as well, and it might be best all round if you don't interfere too much for the moment. It's not worth exhausting yourself by trying to get everything done at the same time.

10 SATURDAY

Moon Age Day 28   Moon Sign Gemini

am . . . .

pm . . . .
Trends encourage you to show your talent for analysis and research now, and you can get a great deal done as far as your practical side is concerned. This is probably a good thing, because in a couple of days life could well slow down significantly. When work is out of the way, make the most of new social possibilities with friends.

11 SUNDAY

Moon Age Day 29   Moon Sign Cancer

am . . . .

pm . . . .
Relationships can now offer rewards, and that little planet Mercury should still be doing you a great many favours from its present position in your solar chart. You can also benefit by keeping up-to-date with the latest fashions and by making sure you stay on course in terms of new technology. Remember – you love technology!

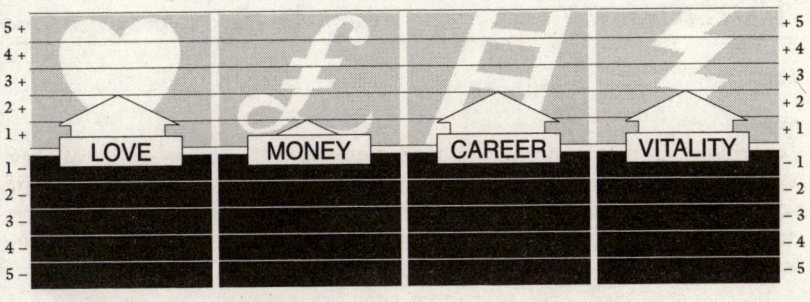

12 MONDAY
Moon Age Day 0   Moon Sign Cancer

am . . . .

pm . . . .
There are signs that things that have been building up for some time can now either be brought to a definite conclusion or else fade away without any real cause. As a result there may be both pleasant and less than pleasant surprises to deal with today. Even when things don't work out as you wish, you can look for sensible alternatives.

13 TUESDAY
Moon Age Day 1   Moon Sign Leo

am . . . .

pm . . . .
This has potential to be a rather sluggish time and one that supports a rather half-hearted approach. It may be difficult to avoid this whilst the lunar low is present, but there is much to be said for relying on others to push situations forward on your behalf. Even if your own personal energy is flagging, the same might not be true of those around you.

14 WEDNESDAY
Moon Age Day 2   Moon Sign Leo

am . . . .

pm . . . .
The planetary lull continues, and it may be difficult to summon up the same level of enthusiasm about life as would generally be the case. Your best response is to be patient with yourself and with the world at large, because the less than favourable trends won't extend far beyond today. A day to look after cash and avoid spending lavishly.

15 THURSDAY
Moon Age Day 3   Moon Sign Virgo

am . . . .

pm . . . .
There are signs that emotional relationships will provide your warmest and most enjoyable contacts for the moment. Look to the people who genuinely know you the best and who will be quite willing to do what it takes to keep you happy. You may also decide to call in a few favours from especially good and cherished friends.

16 FRIDAY   *Moon Age Day 4   Moon Sign Virgo*

am . . . .

pm . . . .
With Mars in its present position it might be wisest to let some situations run their course, whilst you plan for what you want to do next. This period can be something of a watershed, though there may be little you can do to influence life. Such a situation can be frustrating for Aquarius, but you have scope to make progress in the end.

17 SATURDAY   *Moon Age Day 5   Moon Sign Libra*

am . . . .

pm . . . .
You now have an opportunity to tap into favourable circumstances, especially when it comes to your contacts with friends and acquaintances. Your best approach is to plan ahead in order to have something special happening and do whatever you can to get family members motivated for the weekend. Outdoor activities should be a must!

18 SUNDAY   *Moon Age Day 6   Moon Sign Libra*

am . . . .

pm . . . .
At what could well be a very crucial stage of your life, a degree of indecision is a distinct possibility. In order to react more instinctively and positively you will need to recognise that your own thoughts are actually worth something. This might be slightly difficult, particularly if you feel that other people are ignoring your point of view.

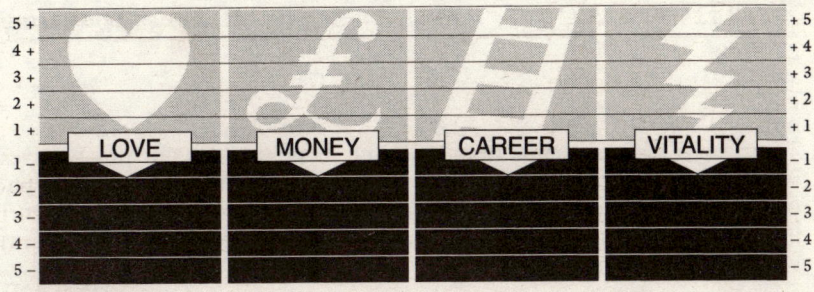

19 MONDAY

Moon Age Day 7   Moon Sign Scorpio

am . . . .

pm . . . .
You need to ensure there is plenty happening in personal attachments and be willing to take part in social events too. One thing that you might decide to put on the back burner for the moment is work, because it all depends on whether you have the time to fit it in. Be ready to find newer and better means of making money in the days to come.

20 TUESDAY

Moon Age Day 8   Moon Sign Scorpio

am . . . .

pm . . . .
Things should be running fairly smoothly for you across the board, and you may not wish to meddle with situations that seem to be working out very well of their own accord. Bear in mind that this could well be down to your efforts in the past. For the moment, why not devote some time to learning and exploring in the way Aquarius must?

21 WEDNESDAY

Moon Age Day 9   Moon Sign Sagittarius

am . . . .

pm . . . .
Even if you find plenty to keep you happy and enthusiastic during the middle of the week, you may not be making the progress you would wish, particularly if other people are proving somehow difficult. Fortunately you can afford to smile at the odd mishap and allow nature to take its course. It's a question of being well in command.

22 THURSDAY

Moon Age Day 10   Moon Sign Sagittarius

am . . . .

pm . . . .
The time is right to define new goals and to be sure of your prospective actions. You now have what it takes to deal swiftly with any challenges to your authority. Persuading other people to follow your lead is very important at this time, and you might actively decide to abandon those who want to go their own way.

23 FRIDAY
Moon Age Day 11   Moon Sign Sagittarius

am . . . .

pm . . . .
More positive opportunities are now available on the monetary front, especially if you are in business. Added securities can be sought from the direction of your partner, and you have scope to make this a very comfortable and more certain time as far as love is concerned. Maybe your expectations are not quite as high as they have been.

24 SATURDAY
Moon Age Day 12   Moon Sign Capricorn

am . . . .

pm . . . .
One-to-one partnerships are once again positively highlighted, encouraging you to spend plenty of time in the company of people you care for deeply. Beware of getting yourself too involved in matters that tax you too much, because in a practical sense you are now better off dealing with the superficial aspects of life.

25 SUNDAY
Moon Age Day 13   Moon Sign Capricorn

am . . . .

pm . . . .
Trends suggest that unexpected setbacks are now possible. The Moon is in your solar twelfth house, making it difficult to be quite as positive and reactive as would normally be the case. It pays to keep an eye on money and leave major financial decisions until tomorrow. Treat today as a short interlude during which you can relax.

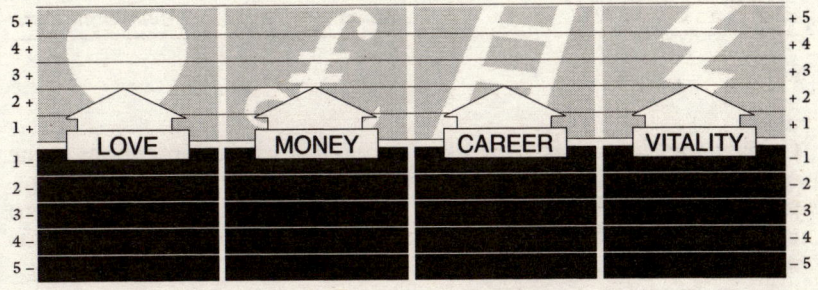

26 MONDAY
Moon Age Day 14   Moon Sign Aquarius

am . . . .

pm . . . .

You seem to have the edge now when it comes to decision-making, and the arrival of the lunar high comes just in time for you to play a major role in new situations that are on offer. It's time to allow any negativity that has surrounded you to blow away on a wind of change, and to ensure you are as reactive and positive as ever.

27 TUESDAY
Moon Age Day 15   Moon Sign Aquarius

am . . . .

pm . . . .

You should be capitalising on positive trends in both your personal and your professional life, and looking for ways to make the most of potentially exciting social possibilities. Travel is well accented at this time and you can benefit from any change of scene, whether it was planned ages ago or has just been decided upon today.

28 WEDNESDAY
Moon Age Day 16   Moon Sign Aquarius

am . . . .

pm . . . .

Aquarius can be very self-sufficient at the moment, and shouldn't require a great deal from the world outside. On the contrary, the emphasis is on making your own decisions and refusing to allow others to interfere in matters you see as being entirely your own. Going it alone is not usually Aquarian, but seems to be right now.

29 THURSDAY
Moon Age Day 17   Moon Sign Pisces

am . . . .

pm . . . .

Gaining the support of co-workers for your goals and intentions is the order of the day. Business and work relationships can be harmonious – possibly more settled than personal ones. This would be an ideal time to invest in new technology or to upgrade some piece of equipment that has been playing up. Look out for a special bargain.

30 FRIDAY

Moon Age Day 18   Moon Sign Pisces

am . . . .

pm . . . .
Favourable highlights continue through personal relationships and your willingness to move around and to make the best of the summer weather. When it comes to impressing people with your natural charm you should have no difficulty whatsoever. You needn't be too quick to pass judgement on the actions of a casual acquaintance.

31 SATURDAY

Moon Age Day 19   Moon Sign Aries

am . . . .

pm . . . .
Tricky decisions may be a natural aspect of your personal life now, and you probably won't want other people to be involved in the process. It could be said that for a day or two you will be quite closed and secretive, which isn't usually the case for Aquarius. People would never guess what you are thinking, but thoughts run deep.

1 SUNDAY

Moon Age Day 20   Moon Sign Aries

am . . . .

pm . . . .
You might find it difficult to be decisive for a few days. It isn't about refusing to get involved or to make decisions, simply about remaining open and flexible in your attitude. This is no bad thing, because there may be circumstances around you now that will probably work out better if you just wait a while. Socially you can be on top form.

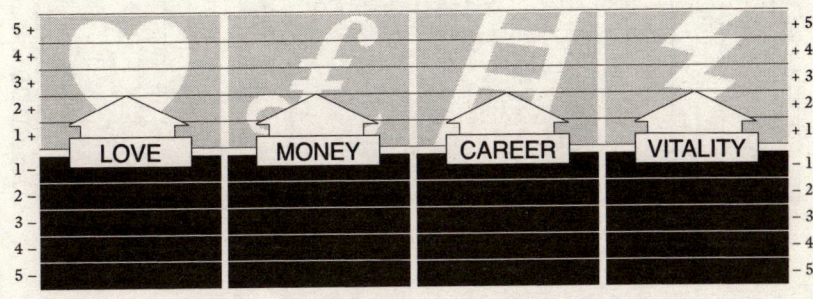

August 2010

YOUR MONTH AT A GLANCE

⊕ = Opportunities are around   ⊖ = Be on the defensive   ⬤ = Life is pretty ordinary

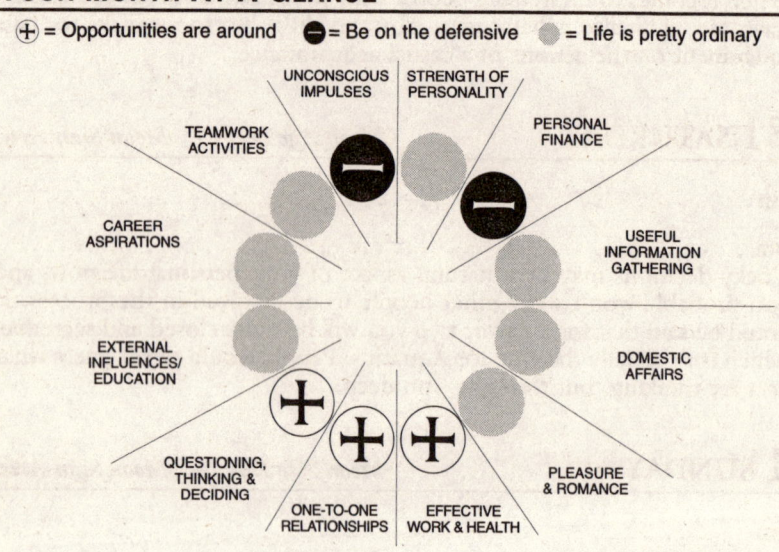

UNCONSCIOUS IMPULSES — ⊖

STRENGTH OF PERSONALITY

PERSONAL FINANCE

TEAMWORK ACTIVITIES

CAREER ASPIRATIONS

USEFUL INFORMATION GATHERING — ⊖

EXTERNAL INFLUENCES/ EDUCATION

DOMESTIC AFFAIRS

QUESTIONING, THINKING & DECIDING — ⊕

ONE-TO-ONE RELATIONSHIPS — ⊕

EFFECTIVE WORK & HEALTH — ⊕

PLEASURE & ROMANCE

AUGUST HIGHS AND LOWS

Here I show you how the rhythms of the Moon will affect you this month. Like the tide, your energies and abilities will rise and fall with its pattern. When it is above the centre line, go for it, when it is below, you should be resting.

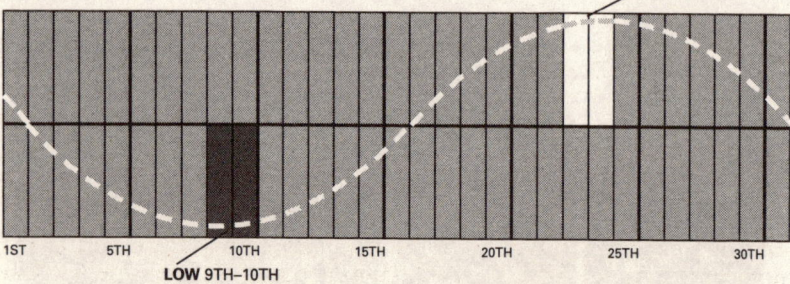

HIGH 23RD–24TH

1ST   5TH   10TH   15TH   20TH   25TH   30TH

LOW 9TH–10TH

2 MONDAY *Moon Age Day 21   Moon Sign Aries*

am . . . .

pm . . . .
Along comes a new phase that can offer you inspirational moments and quite enchanting possibilities. With the Sun now in your solar seventh house you can afford to be open-minded, optimistic and willing to share what you are with the world. This is Aquarius at its best, and you needn't go short of attention or potential new friends.

3 TUESDAY *Moon Age Day 22   Moon Sign Taurus*

am . . . .

pm . . . .
Although you can't convince all of the people all of the time, that might not matter too much today. You should be quite willing to let circumstances mature in such a way that people can see how right you were. This infers a degree of patience on your part that certainly isn't always present in the Aquarian nature as a rule.

4 WEDNESDAY *Moon Age Day 23   Moon Sign Taurus*

am . . . .

pm . . . .
Don't be afraid to enlist the co-operation of colleagues and friends. The input you obtain from others may well light the path towards success. You are at your very best when it comes to sharing, though there may be certain elements of life that you prefer to keep to yourself. This aspect of your nature is unusual – but then so is Aquarius!

5 THURSDAY *Moon Age Day 24   Moon Sign Gemini*

am . . . .

pm . . . .
Today is about feeling free to express yourself, so you would be wise to remove yourself from any situations that are repressive or that go against your own natural inclinations. Nothing could be worse for you at the moment than to feel squashed by circumstances or bullied by people you don't care for.

6 FRIDAY
Moon Age Day 25   Moon Sign Gemini

am ....

pm ....
Your strength lies in your determination to get your views taken on board today, and you shouldn't take no for an answer if you are definitely sure of your ground. However, there's nothing wrong with seeking help from professional experts, and you can learn a great deal as a result. An even-handed approach works best at the moment.

7 SATURDAY
Moon Age Day 26   Moon Sign Cancer

am ....

pm ....
Even if practical matters are going smoothly enough, you need to ask yourself whether you are being a hard taskmaster in terms of what you expect from others. This might be a professional issue or even something at home. Try to make the jobs you hand out as much fun as possible, and balance enjoyment with hard work.

8 SUNDAY
Moon Age Day 27   Moon Sign Cancer

am ....

pm ....
Now you can thrive on contacts with people from very different backgrounds and environments than your own. This is not at all unusual for Aquarius, which loves variety and revels in differences. What a great time this would be to a take a holiday and to experience something totally different from ordinary, everyday life.

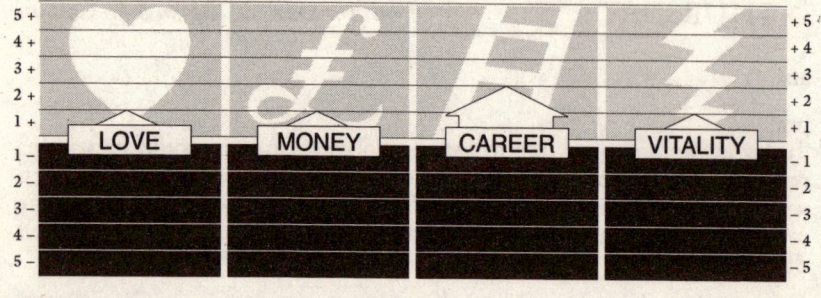

9 MONDAY
Moon Age Day 28   Moon Sign Leo

am . . . .

pm . . . .
You might find it wise to wind down a few of your efforts for a couple of days. The lunar low could take the wind from your sails and make it extra-difficult for you to get what you want from life in a material sense. Fortunately these restrictions are short-lived, though you may also feel out of sorts emotionally at present.

10 TUESDAY
Moon Age Day 0   Moon Sign Leo

am . . . .

pm . . . .
This is not a day for making much in the way of gains, especially in a financial sense. You might have to make do with second-best in some situations, and it may also be quite hard to enlist the support you really need. Later in the day you can improve things and ensure that situations on the personal scene look more positive by the evening.

11 WEDNESDAY
Moon Age Day 1   Moon Sign Virgo

am . . . .

pm . . . .
A new and more profitable period is on offer, especially where your social life is concerned. This is an ideal time for getting to know new people, and you have all it takes to open up important new avenues in friendship. If your love life isn't exactly what you would wish, be prepared to work at creating a little more oomph!

12 THURSDAY
Moon Age Day 2   Moon Sign Virgo

am . . . .

pm . . . .
Involving yourself in a multitude of daily tasks is all very well, though it might mean that you don't have much spare time. That would be a shame because you need space to breathe and to think at the moment. A little oasis of peace should be available to you, but you will have to think about how you can take advantage of it.

13 FRIDAY

Moon Age Day 3   Moon Sign Libra

am . . . .

pm . . . .
Your mind could now be working at super-fast speed, bringing a tendency to express yourself in a rather hurried manner. Bear in mind that mistakes are possible as a result, and you might not be making the best of impressions. It's worth slowing things down a little and making a conscious effort not to run around from pillar to post.

14 SATURDAY

Moon Age Day 4   Moon Sign Libra

am . . . .

pm . . . .
A frank exchange of views could be very advantageous to you at the moment because you will not only learn something new but also let others know the way your mind is really working. You needn't spend too much time being tactful if people have asked for your opinions. Don't allow your capabilities to be underestimated.

15 SUNDAY

Moon Age Day 5   Moon Sign Libra

am . . . .

pm . . . .
Professional opinions are important, though they are not always exciting, or even relevant. In any case this is after all a Sunday, so whether you are working or not you can afford to find at least some time for personal enjoyment. It's time to dump practical concerns for a few hours and find newer and better ways to let your hair down.

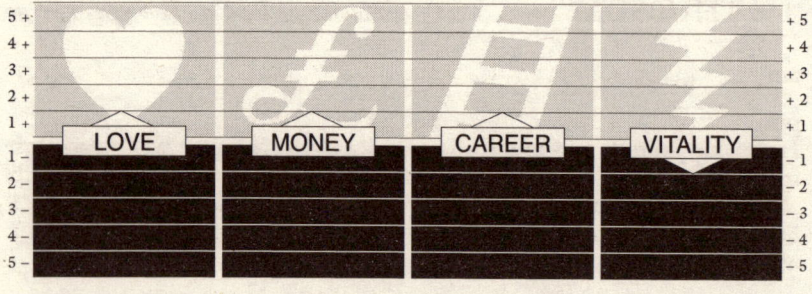

16 MONDAY
Moon Age Day 6   Moon Sign Scorpio

am . . . .

pm . . . .
Conversations with others, though still potentially inspiring and relevant, could also prove to be somewhat fraught at certain stages today. It really depends on the subject matter, so you may decide to keep right away from the deeply personal aspects of life. Beware of raising issues from the past that others are trying to forget!

17 TUESDAY
Moon Age Day 7   Moon Sign Scorpio

am . . . .

pm . . . .
Simple talks to friends are the order of the day, rather than anything too deep, intellectual or philosophical. There are positive trends associated with taking what some might call a superficial view of life. Whilst others get all studious and enmeshed in details, you have what it takes to skip along in bare feet, humming a little tune.

18 WEDNESDAY
Moon Age Day 8   Moon Sign Sagittarius

am . . . .

pm . . . .
Now you can take steps to broaden your mental and physical horizons, though you need do it in your own way and at your own speed. Are you constantly being prodded by relatives or friends who want you to rush? Remember that this is not your best approach right now. Let people marvel at your cool approach to life.

19 THURSDAY
Moon Age Day 9   Moon Sign Sagittarius

am . . . .

pm . . . .
From time to time you are in a position to be a free spirit who is not too flustered or bothered by trivial matters and inconsequential details. Such is the case whilst you have Mars in your solar ninth house. All the king's horses and all his men probably won't make you do anything you don't want today – that's just the way things are.

20 FRIDAY
Moon Age Day 10   Moon Sign Capricorn

am . . . .

pm . . . .
With the Moon entering your solar twelfth house today, a little solitude would be no bad thing. That doesn't mean you have to turn into any sort of hermit, though it's worth spending a few hours on your own, doing whatever needs to be done. On the way you can use the opportunity to think and to mull over some practical possibilities.

21 SATURDAY ☿
Moon Age Day 11   Moon Sign Capricorn

am . . . .

pm . . . .
Personal relationships now offer you scope to find fulfilment, and there is an emphasis on how you present yourself to other people. The time is right to break out, but probably not until Monday. For the moment it pays to play it cool and show someone you are interested, though without going over the top.

22 SUNDAY ☿
Moon Age Day 12   Moon Sign Capricorn

am . . . .

pm . . . .
This is another day during which you can skip along through life, looking and feeling attractive and willing to enjoy whatever is going on around you. Social interaction is well starred, especially at a local level. It's time to make the most of anything that is happening in your vicinity.

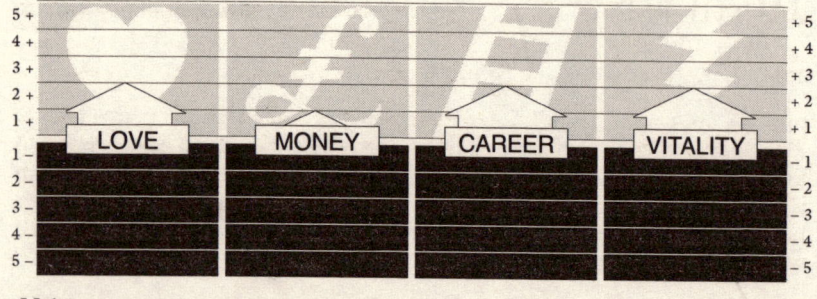

23 MONDAY ☿ *Moon Age Day 13   Moon Sign Aquarius*

am . . . .

pm . . . .
Your intuition is extremely well marked today, and with the lunar high assisting your efforts there is no limit to what you can comfortably achieve. Things may need to change in certain areas, and you will recognise the fact instinctively. Don't be at all surprised if you manage to become flavour of the month in a big way now.

24 TUESDAY ☿ *Moon Age Day 14   Moon Sign Aquarius*

am . . . .

pm . . . .
Today responds best to a far more dynamic and active approach. There are gains to be made in financial terms and you can get Lady Luck on your side when it matters the most. By all means put travel high on your agenda, as this would be an ideal time for a holiday or some sort of short break that is arranged at more or less the last moment.

25 WEDNESDAY ☿ *Moon Age Day 15   Moon Sign Pisces*

am . . . .

pm . . . .
There is much to be said for getting out and about and seeking out interesting people. Some of these individuals, even if they start out as social contacts, could prove to be extremely important to you in a professional or financial way. It's worth cultivating some new interests whilst your energy levels are enhanced.

26 THURSDAY ☿ *Moon Age Day 16   Moon Sign Pisces*

am . . . .

pm . . . .
The pace now picks up and it is important to streamline your life as much as possible. The Sun has now moved into your solar eighth house and this is a sure indication that you need to think about dumping things that are no longer any use to you. With everything to play for in the personal stakes, it pays to make a good impression.

27 FRIDAY ☿ *Moon Age Day 17* *Moon Sign Pisces*

am . . . .

pm . . . .
Seize chances whenever you can and don't be worried if that means
leaving behind something that has been with you for a very long time.
This might be a material possession, but is much more likely to be a
redundant attitude or a judgement about yourself that is far from the
truth. There are good reasons to look after money today.

28 SATURDAY ☿ *Moon Age Day 18* *Moon Sign Aries*

am . . . .

pm . . . .
There are strong signs that you might get yourself involved in arguments
around this time. It won't help your case to fall out with people, and with
a little of that Aquarian tact it can easily be avoided. Make sure you find
something interesting to do, especially later in the day. You should
certainly not sit at home and knit!

29 SUNDAY ☿ *Moon Age Day 19* *Moon Sign Aries*

am . . . .

pm . . . .
If you take your own ideas and opinions too much for granted you could
fall out with others as a result. There is definitely a way to get what you
want, whilst at the same time convincing those around you that you have
listened very carefully to their opinions. In any case, compromise might
not turn out to be a bad thing.

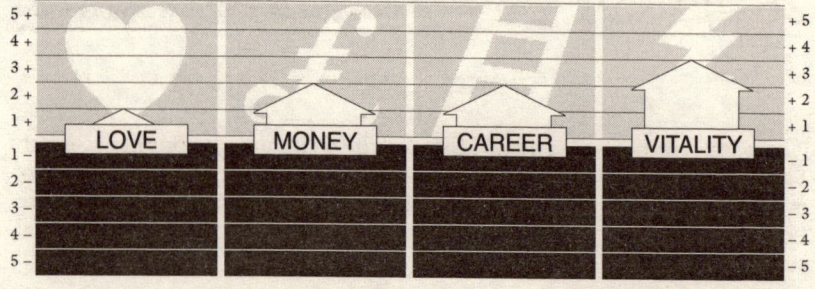

30 MONDAY   ☿   *Moon Age Day 20*   *Moon Sign Taurus*

am . . . .

pm . . . .
Planetary influences now show that there are benefits to be had from joint plans, including those that relate to money. This is also a favourable period for intimacy with loved ones and especially with your partner. If you have recently begun a romantic attachment you should now be in a position to increase the intensity.

31 TUESDAY   ☿   *Moon Age Day 21*   *Moon Sign Taurus*

am . . . .

pm . . . .
The time is right to abandon anything that is not working and start again from scratch. To some people this would either be frightening or a real chore, but not to you. Aquarius needs change like it needs air, and with the Sun in its present position this becomes possible. In business matters an active and enterprising approach works now.

1 WEDNESDAY   ☿   *Moon Age Day 22*   *Moon Sign Gemini*

am . . . .

pm . . . .
With Mars in its present position the focus is on your dislike for restrictions, especially when it comes to your personal freedom. You may well fight like a tiger if anyone tries to pin you down and probably won't take kindly to people telling you how things should be done. You are a free spirit and have a chance to prove it today.

2 THURSDAY   ☿   *Moon Age Day 23*   *Moon Sign Gemini*

am . . . .

pm . . . .
Don't be afraid to review and alter your ambitions constantly this week. This doesn't make you fickle, it merely indicates that your mind is working all the time and that there are many possibilities available. Trends encourage Aquarians to focus on travel over great distances, whether for work or for pleasure.

3 FRIDAY ☿ *Moon Age Day 24   Moon Sign Cancer*

am . . . .

pm . . . .
This is a time when, on the whole, you have scope to make some important changes that have a bearing on your social life. These need not lead you away from what you already enjoy, but might make it better still. You can be very inventive at the moment, and have the ability to derive more than one benefit from any action you take.

4 SATURDAY ☿ *Moon Age Day 25   Moon Sign Cancer*

am . . . .

pm . . . .
Progressive trends continue and especially in the workplace for those Aquarians who work at the weekend. If your time is your own this is an ideal interlude to do things at home that could make it more comfortable in the longer term. If you have DIY on your mind, why not seek some expert advice before you start?

5 SUNDAY ☿ *Moon Age Day 26   Moon Sign Leo*

am . . . .

pm . . . .
A little careful thought is necessary before you embark on anything too energetic today. With the lunar low around it may be difficult to find the energy you need, and in any case you would be wise not to get too deeply enmeshed in anything complicated. Better by far to put your feet up and to have a relaxing day.

5 +			+ 5
4 +			+ 4
3 +			+ 3
2 +			+ 2
1 +			+ 1
LOVE	MONEY	CAREER	VITALITY
1 –			– 1
2 –			– 2
3 –			– 3
4 –			– 4
5 –			– 5

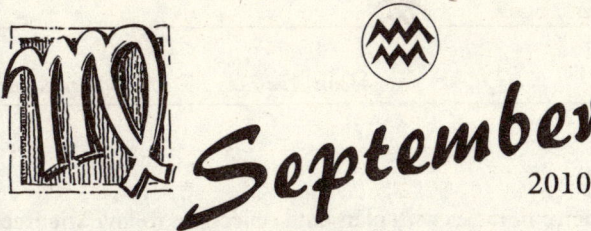

September 2010

YOUR MONTH AT A GLANCE

⊕ = Opportunities are around ⊖ = Be on the defensive ⬤ = Life is pretty ordinary

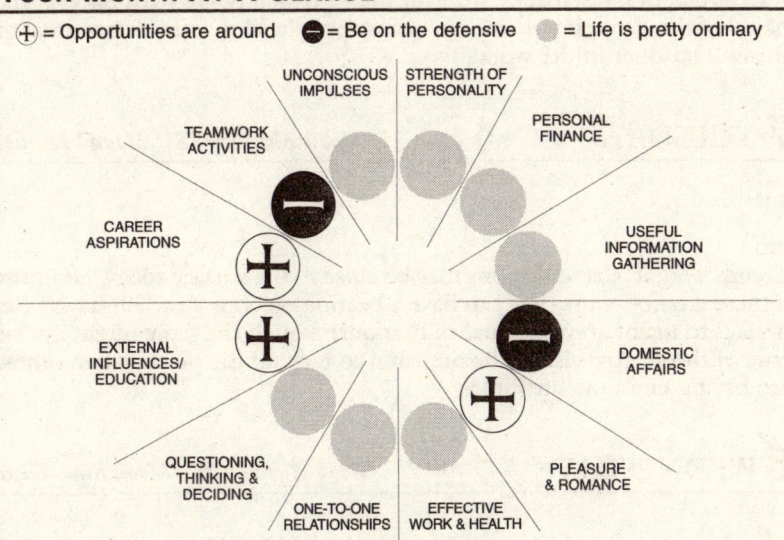

UNCONSCIOUS IMPULSES
STRENGTH OF PERSONALITY
PERSONAL FINANCE
TEAMWORK ACTIVITIES
CAREER ASPIRATIONS
USEFUL INFORMATION GATHERING
EXTERNAL INFLUENCES/ EDUCATION
DOMESTIC AFFAIRS
QUESTIONING, THINKING & DECIDING
PLEASURE & ROMANCE
ONE-TO-ONE RELATIONSHIPS
EFFECTIVE WORK & HEALTH

SEPTEMBER HIGHS AND LOWS

Here I show you how the rhythms of the Moon will affect you this month. Like the tide, your energies and abilities will rise and fall with its pattern. When it is above the centre line, go for it, when it is below, you should be resting.

HIGH 19TH–20TH

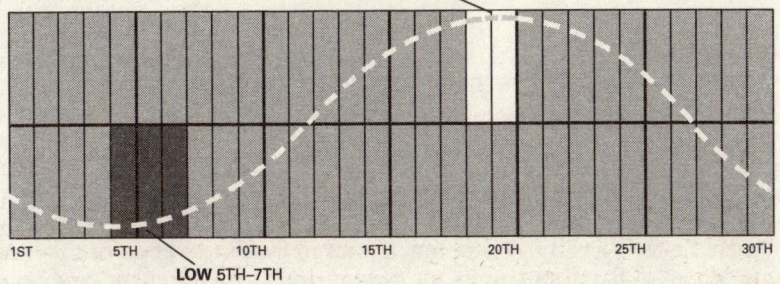

1ST 5TH 10TH 15TH 20TH 25TH 30TH

LOW 5TH–7TH

121

6 MONDAY ☿ *Moon Age Day 27   Moon Sign Leo*

am . . . .

pm . . . .
Don't expect to achieve miracles with plans and objectives today. The fact
is that with the lunar low around it's simply a question of holding your
own. Temporary setbacks are a distinct possibility, and patience is the
name of the game if you are up against people who seem determined to
throw a spanner in the works.

7 TUESDAY ☿ *Moon Age Day 28   Moon Sign Leo*

am . . . .

pm . . . .
Trends suggest that emotions may be close to the surface today, and even
if these are not yours they can have a bearing on your day. You have what
it takes to maintain your sense of humour, though the same might not be
true of those around you. Be prepared to pick up the pieces when others
are having emotional trouble.

8 WEDNESDAY ☿ *Moon Age Day 0·   Moon Sign Virgo*

am . . . .

pm . . . .
This has potential to be a day of reorganisation and renewal. The lunar
low is out of the way and the chief planetary influence is that of the Sun
in your solar eighth house. Now is the time to get rid of whatever is
redundant in your life, and you can afford to be quite ruthless about the
way you decide that enough is enough in some senses.

9 THURSDAY ☿ *Moon Age Day 1   Moon Sign Virgo*

am . . . .

pm . . . .
An optimistic and light-hearted interlude is on offer – and thank
goodness! The planet Venus can be especially useful to you at the
moment, assisting you to bring much joy and happiness into your life. A
high degree of freedom counts for a great deal at the moment, and you
probably won't respond well to anyone who tries to hold you back.

10 FRIDAY ☿ *Moon Age Day 2 Moon Sign Libra*

am . . . .

pm . . . .
Be ready to offer advice if it is sought around now. There are good reasons for this, because even if you have made some serious gaffes regarding your own life, you can ensure that the advice you give to others is generally very sound. In social matters this is an ideal time to act on impulse and also to plan for a special weekend.

11 SATURDAY ☿ *Moon Age Day 3 Moon Sign Libra*

am . . . .

pm . . . .
Generally speaking you should be well able to take care of what is yours around now. Although you aren't usually a selfish sort, there's nothing wrong with protecting your investments in a number of ways, nor with challenging anyone who seeks to interfere in your practical life. Socially speaking, make sure you are riding high at present.

12 SUNDAY ☿ *Moon Age Day 4 Moon Sign Scorpio*

am . . . .

pm . . . .
Close ties to others can be strengthened whilst the Sun retains its present position in your solar chart. However, this is also a time for change and one that might demand quite a lot from you in terms of courage. You need to be willing to make the sort of alterations to your life that could be quite worrying at first.

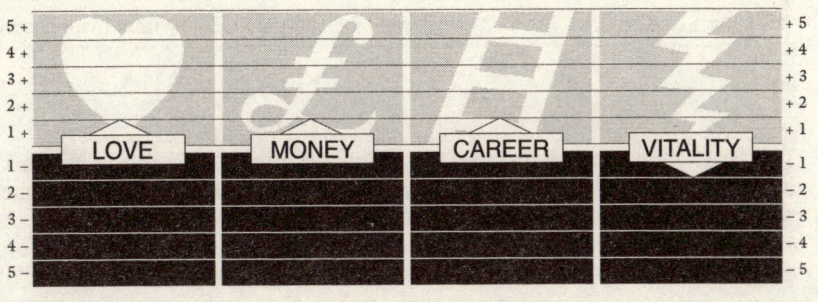

13 MONDAY ☿ *Moon Age Day 5   Moon Sign Scorpio*

am . . . .

pm . . . .
There is much to be said for pursuing career developments at this time.
You should be a good deal clearer about your objectives and you needn't
shy away from the sort of changes that might have seemed extremely
unlikely only a very short time ago. Acting on impulse is natural for you,
but counts for a great deal now in a social sense.

14 TUESDAY *Moon Age Day 6   Moon Sign Sagittarius*

am . . . .

pm . . . .
Now is a favourable time to consolidate, to organise your affairs and to
rearrange your living situation in some way. You have what it takes to cut
through any amount of red tape and to get on well with all practicalities.
On the way you can be of tremendous help to other people, especially
anyone who has been rather confused of late.

15 WEDNESDAY *Moon Age Day 7   Moon Sign Sagittarius*

am . . . .

pm . . . .
There may be a tendency to feel somewhat unsettled, but that's not
surprising with Mercury as well as the Sun now in your eighth house. You
needn't allow minor setbacks to dishearten you because some of these
might not turn out to be setbacks at all. Even when you are on the right
road, it's natural sometimes to think you are lost.

16 THURSDAY *Moon Age Day 8   Moon Sign Capricorn*

am . . . .

pm . . . .
You are presently best suited to doing things that keep you fully
occupied, especially in a work sense. If you have been at all dissatisfied
with your career in the recent past, now could be the best time to look
around for something different. Make the most of the good luck that is
on your side and your knack of making yourself popular with people.

17 FRIDAY
Moon Age Day 9   Moon Sign Capricorn

am . . . .

pm . . . .
Personal matters might have a bearing on your capabilities in the outside world, and you would be wise to keep the two as separate as possible. Be prepared to listen carefully to anything that is said to you now that comes like a bolt from the blue. The focus is on a slightly untypical timid tendency for a day or two.

18 SATURDAY
Moon Age Day 10   Moon Sign Capricorn

am . . . .

pm . . . .
It could be the position of the Moon that is supporting a slightly jumpy interlude, though you needn't let this last beyond today. Indeed as the hours pass on this particular Saturday you should be willing to become more and more positive and determined in your attitude. It pays to be with friends as much as possible today.

19 SUNDAY
Moon Age Day 11   Moon Sign Aquarius

am . . . .

pm . . . .
The lunar high gives you scope to do well in pioneering ventures, and any tendency to be hesitant should now be out of the window. There is a chance to enlarge your personal horizons, and you should have no difficulty when it comes to making the best of impressions on others. You can afford to chance your arm on occasions today.

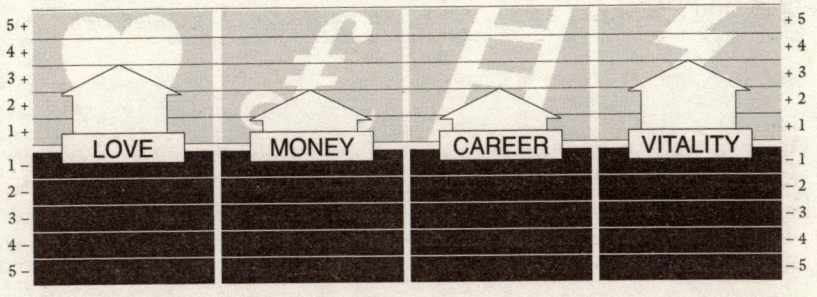

20 MONDAY
Moon Age Day 12   Moon Sign Aquarius

am . . . .

pm . . . .

Lady Luck can assist you with your most important decisions at the start of this particular week, and you have everything you need to persuade others to follow you anywhere. It should be full steam ahead as far as your career is concerned, and getting your own way should be a natural aspect of your life now.

21 TUESDAY
Moon Age Day 13   Moon Sign Pisces

am . . . .

pm . . . .

The Sun will be moving on in a day or two and this is the last chance to sort things out in a big way. September is late in the year for a spring-clean, but this is still possible, either in your home or in your mind. Be willing to throw away anything that is no longer any use to you. This includes outmoded concepts and pointless worries.

22 WEDNESDAY
Moon Age Day 14   Moon Sign Pisces

am . . . .

pm . . . .

Venus has sped on to your solar tenth house from where it exerts a very positive influence, especially in a career sense. It also assists you to get your own way with partners and even senior figures. Any Aquarians who have been considering a long journey could find this an ideal period for finalising plans.

23 THURSDAY
Moon Age Day 15   Moon Sign Pisces

am . . . .

pm . . . .

Do you feel you are having to fight to get ahead in some way? Bear in mind that the effort should be worthwhile, especially when it comes to finances and personal objectives. Not everyone might be on your side at this time but you can persuade people to come good for you when it matters most. New adventures now become possible.

24 FRIDAY
Moon Age Day 16   Moon Sign Aries

am . . . .

pm . . . .
Travel issues should help you to put a smile on your face and give you something to think about that is potentially exciting. This is important because a dull life with nothing in store is not to be recommended. Actually there could be plenty going on, though you will have to think hard in order to realise exactly what your opportunities are now.

25 SATURDAY
Moon Age Day 17   Moon Sign Aries

am . . . .

pm . . . .
Be ready to capitalise on a few days of smooth progress with very little in the way of waves to buffet you around. In some ways this is great, though in others it might seem quite tedious. Aquarius is often ready to complain when things are going topsy-turvy, though in reality you enjoy the cut and thrust of a complicated life.

26 SUNDAY
Moon Age Day 18   Moon Sign Taurus

am . . . .

pm . . . .
A busy interlude is indicated at the moment, and getting on with your life is the name of the game. This will only be a problem if others are putting their problems on your shoulders and not helping you out. By all means take on a certain amount of responsibility for relatives and friends, but there comes a time when people have to manage.

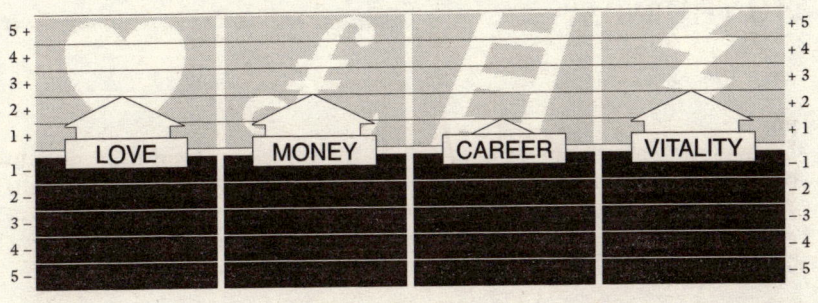

27 MONDAY
Moon Age Day 19   Moon Sign Taurus

am . . . .

pm . . . .
Whilst it is important to keep your long-term goals in sight, the time is also right to spend periods thinking about play and enjoyment right now. The pleasures of family life could be especially appealing and rewarding this week, and now that the Sun has moved on you might also be in the market for a change of scenery and some travel.

28 TUESDAY
Moon Age Day 20   Moon Sign Taurus

am . . . .

pm . . . .
One of your greatest talents is your ability to tune in to the deepest emotional signals that come from other people. This particular skill is especially emphasised around now. It's time to surprise people by knowing exactly what is going in on their heads, maybe even a short while before they realise it themselves!

29 WEDNESDAY
Moon Age Day 21   Moon Sign Gemini

am . . . .

pm . . . .
The spotlight is on your strong concern for getting things done today, mostly in a practical way. Whether or not you can enlist the support of others remains to be seen, but one fact is certain: whether they help you or not, you should be willing to move on anyway. Woe betide anyone who interferes with your choices at this time.

30 THURSDAY
Moon Age Day 22   Moon Sign Gemini

am . . . .

pm . . . .
Leisure and entertainment may be just the tonic you need right now in order to prevent you from taking yourself or anyone else too seriously. Your patient side is not well marked for the moment, and you could so easily fall out with people you see as being unreasonable in any way. There's nothing wrong with standing up for the underdog.

1 FRIDAY
Moon Age Day 23   Moon Sign Cancer

am . . . .

pm . . . .
The sense of security that has been available to you for a while now could be looking slightly shaky, though you need not worry just because you are standing on a wobbly stone today. You may have to spend more time building surer foundations, but that is probably something you can do without thinking. Meanwhile you can still have fun.

2 SATURDAY
Moon Age Day 24   Moon Sign Cancer

am . . . .

pm . . . .
Are your obligations towards others proving to be something of a trial at the moment? One possible option is to decide to allow them to do whatever they choose instead. Of course this state of affairs shouldn't last, and you can still end up running the show. You can't help getting involved, even if you promise yourself you will not do so.

3 SUNDAY
Moon Age Day 25   Moon Sign Leo

am . . . .

pm . . . .
There may be things around that will try your patience today, but these are linked to the arrival of the lunar low. Most of the worries that might seem to be gathering around you have little or no substance, so it's not worth taking too much notice of them. A day to keep busy and active because this month's lunar low is little more than a sham.

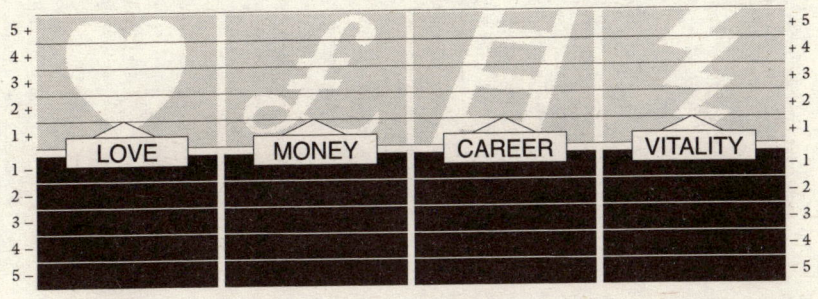

October
2010

YOUR MONTH AT A GLANCE

⊕ = Opportunities are around   ⊖ = Be on the defensive   ⬤ = Life is pretty ordinary

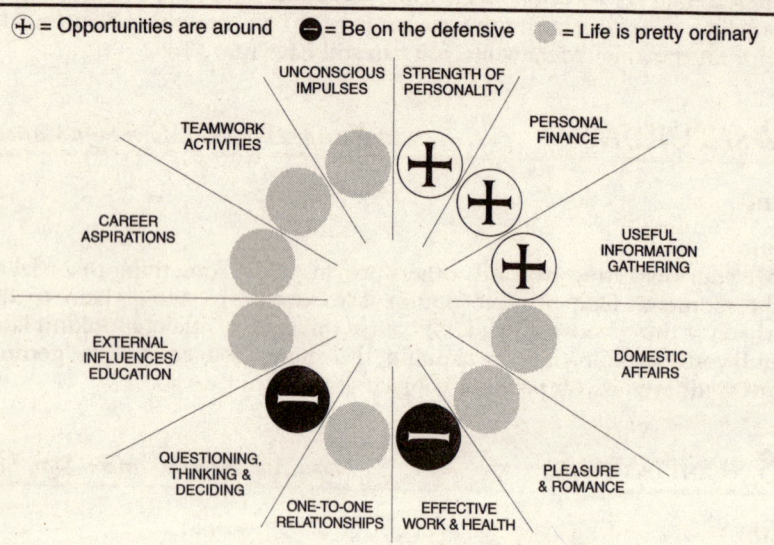

OCTOBER HIGHS AND LOWS

Here I show you how the rhythms of the Moon will affect you this month. Like the tide, your energies and abilities will rise and fall with its pattern. When it is above the centre line, go for it, when it is below, you should be resting.

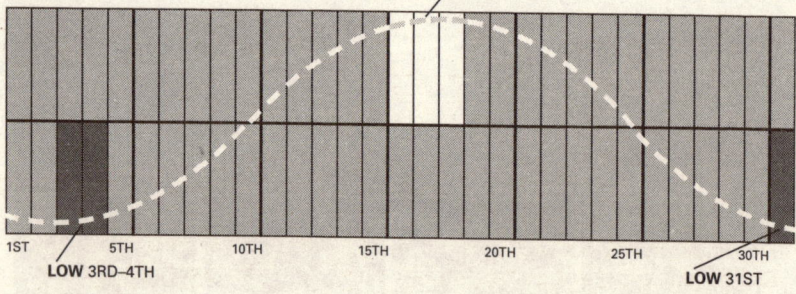

130

4 MONDAY
Moon Age Day 26   Moon Sign Leo

am . . . .

pm . . . .
This is not an ideal time for new ambitions, since the lunar low has potential to get in the way of your best-laid plans. Better by far for the moment to watch and wait, allowing others to stand in the limelight for a while. When you do reappear tomorrow you can ensure it is with all guns blazing, and then you can really get what you want from life!

5 TUESDAY
Moon Age Day 27   Moon Sign Virgo

am . . . .

pm . . . .
Business dealings and emotional relationships now offer you opportunities to look at things rather more deeply, even if you are quite definite and assertive at this time. You can afford to trust your hunches today because your intuition appears to be very strong and it shouldn't let you down when it matters the most.

6 WEDNESDAY
Moon Age Day 28   Moon Sign Virgo

am . . . .

pm . . . .
This is a favourable time for studies or mental interests. It's a question of expanding your horizons and making the most of your ability to get things right first time. New insights and understandings are available, and you have what it takes to turn heads in social settings. How could anyone ignore such a fascinating person as you are?

7 THURSDAY
Moon Age Day 29   Moon Sign Libra

am . . . .

pm . . . .
Freedom could well be the most important thing you have now. It doesn't matter how secure your future looks and how comfortable you feel at work and home, because if you don't feel able to do what you really want everything else is a bit of a sham. Make space to breathe and ensure people understand your needs.

8 FRIDAY

Moon Age Day 0   Moon Sign Libra

am . . . .

pm . . . .
This could be the time for a complete change of scenery, especially when it comes to your social life. Trends encourage you to surround yourself with a variety of people who can each offer you something different. Getting through work shouldn't be hard now, and you are well able to apply yourself, though variety is the key when the work is done.

9 SATURDAY

Moon Age Day 1   Moon Sign Scorpio

am . . . .

pm . . . .
A stimulating mental environment is the order of the day. In fact, the more stimulating it is the better you can operate. Even if you are forced to think about matters that haven't been an issue before, you can do so quite easily as long as you don't feel pressured by mundane events and situations. Variety continues to be the spice of life for you.

10 SUNDAY

Moon Age Day 2   Moon Sign Scorpio

am . . . .

pm . . . .
When it comes to professional matters, you would be wise to take care when you are around superiors or colleagues who have some kind of axe to grind. If you don't work at the weekends this shouldn't be an issue, and it has to be said that the social trends look very favourable indeed. Once again this is a chance to get something new up and running.

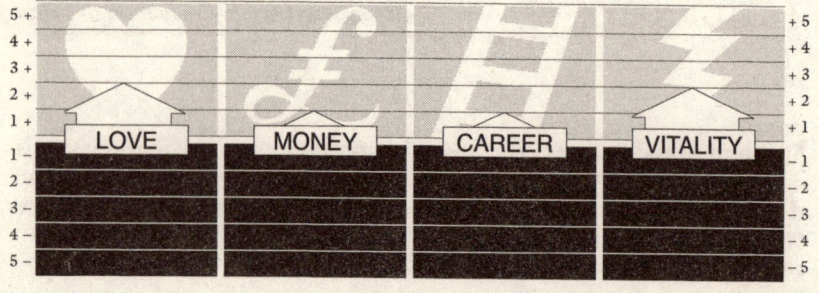

11 MONDAY
Moon Age Day 3   Moon Sign Sagittarius

am . . . .

pm . . . .
Aquarius is naturally very socially oriented, with a great joy for life and a desire to do something different as often as possible. Nothing changes these facts, and they count for a great deal under present planetary trends. Today you operate best when surrounded by as many different types of people as proves to be possible.

12 TUESDAY
Moon Age Day 4   Moon Sign Sagittarius

am . . . .

pm . . . .
There are good reasons to widen your personal horizons as much as possible, and not to restrict yourself just because you feel others may not approve. In reality you have what it takes to be the most approachable and likeable person imaginable. Just bear this in mind and believe it. This should help you to give of your best in every situation.

13 WEDNESDAY
Moon Age Day 5   Moon Sign Sagittarius

am . . . .

pm . . . .
There is likely to be a strong emphasis on work at this time, though getting what you want might be relatively easy in almost any situation. This is because you can combine a very determined attitude with innate kindness and a psychological approach. Few people should deny you any reasonable request if you ask nicely.

14 THURSDAY
Moon Age Day 6   Moon Sign Capricorn

am . . . .

pm . . . .
Today works best if you make sure you are approachable and display your sincerity and your disarming attitude. Don't be at all surprised if you discover you have an admirer you didn't suspect, because you have what it takes to turn heads. If routines prove to be something of a bore, why not try to avoid them?

15 FRIDAY
Moon Age Day 7   Moon Sign Capricorn

am . . . .

pm . . . .
Extended travel and an ability to mix with like-minded people could be important factors in your life now and across the weekend. If circumstances keep you in one place you can at least take a journey in your mind, which with a mind like yours has potential to be nearly as fulfilling. Be prepared to respond to good news from your partner.

16 SATURDAY
Moon Age Day 8   Moon Sign Aquarius

am . . . .

pm . . . .
The Moon is now back in your zodiac sign, supporting a very positive sort of weekend and some quite dynamic actions on your part. By all means rely on your luck, which should be available today in all spheres of your life. In reality you can make much of your own good fortune by doing the right things and being in the right places.

17 SUNDAY
Moon Age Day 9   Moon Sign Aquarius

am . . . .

pm . . . .
Today is about keeping things running smoothly and about doing not only everything that is expected of you but a great deal more too. Motivating other people should be as easy today as it has been across the last week or more, and you have scope to elicit positive responses, mainly because of the way you approach people and situations.

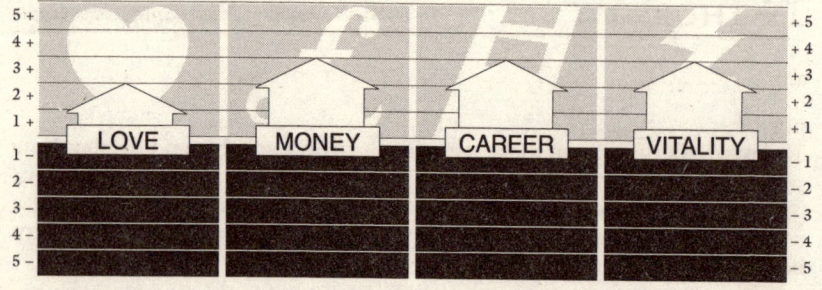

18 MONDAY   *Moon Age Day 10   Moon Sign Aquarius*

am . . . .

pm . . . .
This would be an ideal time to seek support and approval for monetary initiatives from all manner of people, and the start of this particular working week should have much to recommend it. Beware of getting involved in personal arguments about situations that don't matter in the slightest. Principles are fine, but are sometimes overplayed.

19 TUESDAY   *Moon Age Day 11   Moon Sign Pisces*

am . . . .

pm . . . .
The Sun remains in your solar ninth house for the next few days and continues to emphasise travel. If you can't go too far, why not at least look at something new? Try an art gallery or a museum and feed your intellect, which is always a good thing for Aquarius. Today is also favourable for starting new projects and making new friends.

20 WEDNESDAY   *Moon Age Day 12   Moon Sign Pisces*

am . . . .

pm . . . .
The urge for challenge and change is to the fore, and might come along when you least expect it to do so. Do you also get the feeling that someone or something is trying to block your path at an important place? This probably isn't the case, though if you have become hung up on personal freedom you might be tempted to over-react.

21 THURSDAY   *Moon Age Day 13   Moon Sign Aries*

am . . . .

pm . . . .
Happy dialogues seem to be on offer, giving you chance to show how well you get on with most people. Things are changing though, and with Venus in your solar tenth house it is co-operation that brings new situations and possibilities into your life. You may also be looking at an old attachment in a new way, leading to a little nostalgia.

22 FRIDAY
Moon Age Day 14   Moon Sign Aries

am . . . .

pm . . . .
Don't miss out on anything important at work. If you are between positions at this time it's worth concentrating your efforts now and being prepared to look in rather unusual places. If people are relying on you to do the right thing, as always you come good and impress them. You can get everyone to be your friend at the moment.

23 SATURDAY
Moon Age Day 15   Moon Sign Aries

am . . . .

pm . . . .
When it comes to life as a whole you now have the ability to thrive in situations that make demands of you, thanks to your love for the cut and thrust of life. Trends assist you to bring originality to all proceedings and to show others what a very unusual and unpredictable individual you are. There's no harm at all in keeping people guessing.

24 SUNDAY
Moon Age Day 16   Moon Sign Taurus

am . . . .

pm . . . .
Long-term ambitions now come under the spotlight and this is because the Sun has moved on in your solar chart. Career-related issues are also highlighted, and this would be an opportune time to plan something original and even slightly amazing in a social sense. When it comes to assessing the nature of new individuals, use your intuition!

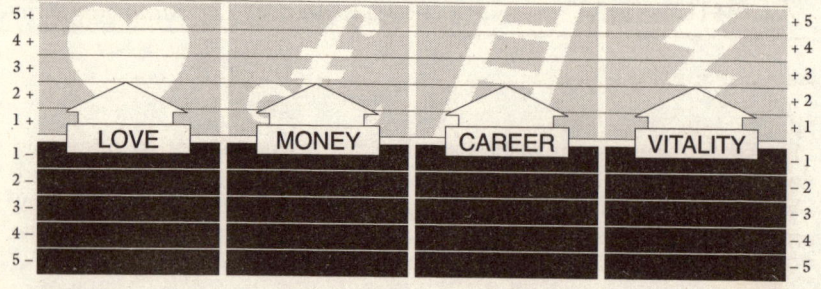

25 MONDAY　　　　*Moon Age Day 17　　Moon Sign Taurus*

am . . . .

pm . . . .
Your personal charm can now have a strong impact on others, and you
have scope to use it to your advantage in a career sense. Your ego is
highlighted at the start of this week, encouraging you to seek attention,
but that's fine if you temper this with plenty of fun. There's nothing
wrong with having people hanging on your every word.

26 TUESDAY　　　　*Moon Age Day 18　　Moon Sign Gemini*

am . . . .

pm . . . .
With so many tenth-house influences in your solar chart at the moment,
your strength lies in your ability to get on well with people at all levels.
Not that this is too surprising, because Aquarius can be one of the
quirkiest and yet the most interesting of all zodiac signs. If people think
you are slightly eccentric, so much the better.

27 WEDNESDAY　　　　*Moon Age Day 19　　Moon Sign Gemini*

am . . . .

pm . . . .
Bear in mind that some people might be slightly threatened by your style
of business or by the fact that you rush in where angels fear to tread.
Taking a few risks at this time is all very well, though you need to ensure
they are quite calculated. If you can't take everyone with you in your
plans, you may decide to let them move along at their own speed.

28 THURSDAY　　　　*Moon Age Day 20　　Moon Sign Cancer*

am . . . .

pm . . . .
In most situations Aquarius moves at its own pace and allows others to
do the same, though there may be situations today in which you have to
take other people's needs into account. This might be something of a
problem. On the one hand you probably want to make progress, but on
the other you could be pricked by your strong conscience.

29 FRIDAY
Moon Age Day 21   Moon Sign Cancer

am . . . .

pm . . . .
It pays to focus on your professional goals and ideals during this period and to ensure they take on a more positive dimension than they have done recently. At the end of this working week you need to be fully on the ball and ready to achieve what you want in every way. A selfish streak may also be apparent, which is unusual for Aquarius.

30 SATURDAY
Moon Age Day 22   Moon Sign Cancer

am . . . .

pm . . . .
Be prepared to stand by your decisions, even if one or two of them look in some sort of doubt. If you are willing to back your hunches you stand the best chance of winning through in the end. It's time to reassess social situations of which you are a part, and to decide whether the time is right to invent something new and interesting.

31 SUNDAY
Moon Age Day 23   Moon Sign Leo

am . . . .

pm . . . .
You would be wise to keep to well-trodden paths today. The lunar low does nothing to lift your spirits, so the going may well be tough. Even the easiest of tasks might take on a new and sometimes disturbing dimension, though not if you are willing to enlist the support of people who have professional or personal skills that you do not.

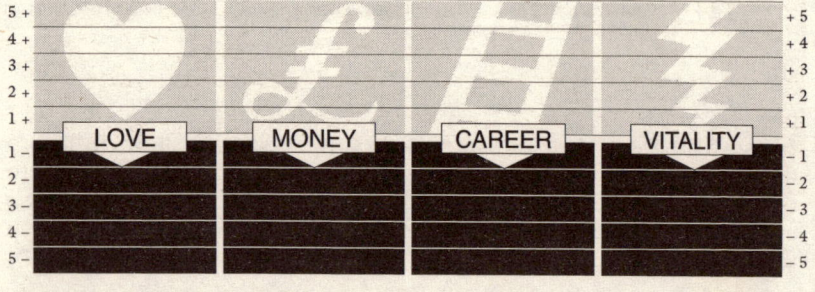

November
2010

YOUR MONTH AT A GLANCE

⊕ = Opportunities are around   ⊖ = Be on the defensive   ⬤ = Life is pretty ordinary

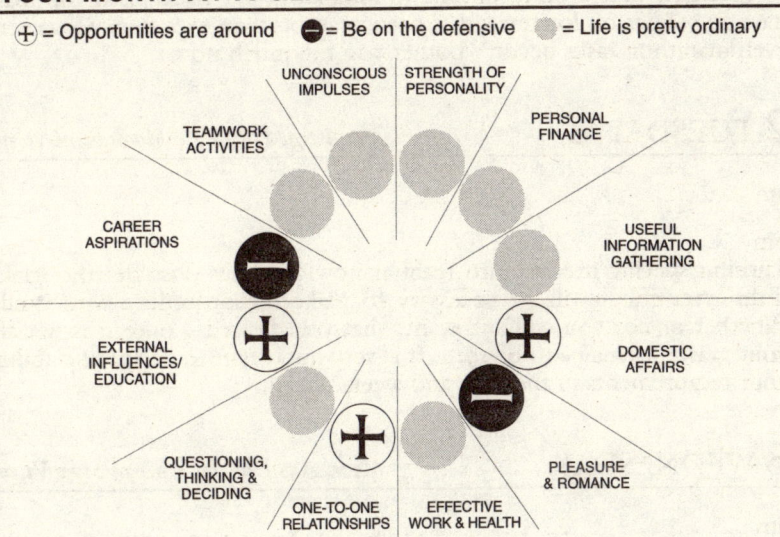

UNCONSCIOUS IMPULSES
STRENGTH OF PERSONALITY
PERSONAL FINANCE
TEAMWORK ACTIVITIES
CAREER ASPIRATIONS
USEFUL INFORMATION GATHERING
EXTERNAL INFLUENCES/ EDUCATION
DOMESTIC AFFAIRS
QUESTIONING, THINKING & DECIDING
ONE-TO-ONE RELATIONSHIPS
EFFECTIVE WORK & HEALTH
PLEASURE & ROMANCE

NOVEMBER HIGHS AND LOWS

Here I show you how the rhythms of the Moon will affect you this month. Like the tide, your energies and abilities will rise and fall with its pattern. When it is above the centre line, go for it, when it is below, you should be resting.

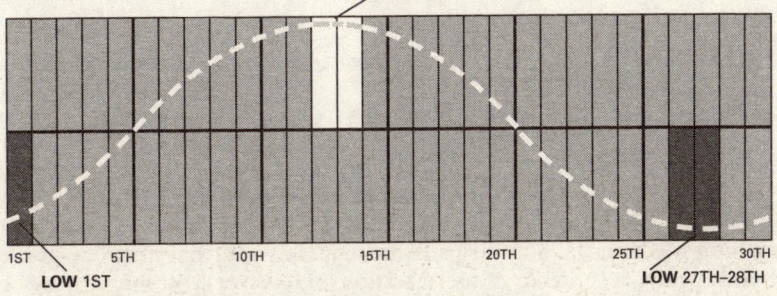

HIGH 13TH–14TH

1ST   5TH   10TH   15TH   20TH   25TH   30TH

LOW 1ST

LOW 27TH–28TH

1 MONDAY
Moon Age Day 24   Moon Sign Leo

am . . . .

pm . . . .
Despite the continuing lunar low, the first day of November offers a period of change and re-evaluation that could prove to be very important to your life. This is an ideal time to look at money issues, and you may have to soldier on longer with a particular job than expected. However, even marathon tasks needn't bother you too much now.

2 TUESDAY
Moon Age Day 25   Moon Sign Virgo

am . . . .

pm . . . .
Turning specific dreams into realities now becomes possible, though a little extra effort will be necessary to make the procedure work well. Whether or not you will still want what you desired – once it is within your grasp – remains to be seen. It is very important to be specific about your requirements in the days and weeks ahead.

3 WEDNESDAY
Moon Age Day 26   Moon Sign Virgo

am . . . .

pm . . . .
Trends suggest that professional demands could be many and varied at this stage of the week, and you may have to work quite hard in order to fulfil expectations. This needn't trouble you too much, as long as you ensure that there are periods during the day when you can do what takes your fancy. All work and no play is bad for Aquarius.

4 THURSDAY
Moon Age Day 27   Moon Sign Libra

am . . . .

pm . . . .
Mars has now moved on in your solar chart and its present position emphasises the more provocative side of your nature. There isn't anything too unusual about this because it is in your nature to push the bounds of the acceptable in social settings. However, you might now be quite outrageous, even by your own Aquarian standards.

5 FRIDAY
Moon Age Day 28   Moon Sign Libra

am . . . .

pm . . . .
Your career could prove to be the most important and possibly also the most interesting sphere of your life today. This doesn't mean you are lacking when it comes to having a good time. Your ability to mix business with pleasure has probably never been so well starred, and this would be an ideal time to turn colleagues into good friends.

6 SATURDAY
Moon Age Day 0   Moon Sign Scorpio

am . . . .

pm . . . .
Progress is possible today if you ensure that others are paying you plenty of attention. If you are at work this will be superiors or colleagues, whereas if you are at home it is likely to be relatives and friends. Being popular is important to you at present, and you might be willing to move mountains in your efforts to prove how amazing you are.

7 SUNDAY
Moon Age Day 1   Moon Sign Scorpio

am . . . .

pm . . . .
It looks as though your popularity is still going to be a major issue. However, you need to ask yourself whether you are trying too hard, which really isn't necessary. Just relax and be yourself. When it comes to romance it's a question of getting into the swing of things and showing how attractive you are. A day to look after the pennies.

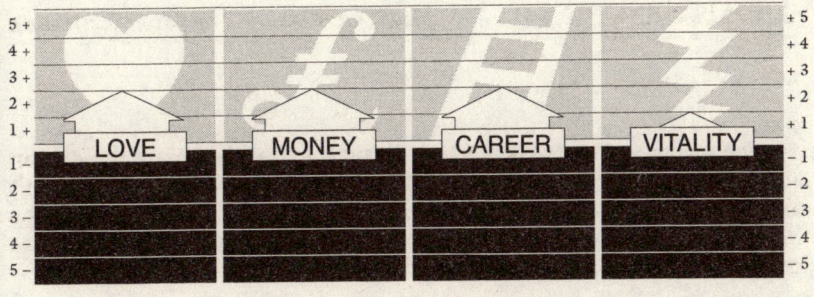

8 MONDAY

Moon Age Day 2   Moon Sign Sagittarius

am . . . .

pm . . . .
Now you have an opportunity to raise your profile in a social sense, and the present position of Mars encourages you to help out if people have specific needs. When it comes to speaking in a public setting your skills are to the fore, and this is no time to underestimate your own capabilities, either professional or personal.

9 TUESDAY

Moon Age Day 3   Moon Sign Sagittarius

am . . . .

pm . . . .
There are gains to be made from involving yourself as much as possible in group activities and getting together with people who have similar views to your own. Not that there should be any trouble in adapting to different types, but your greatest successes at the moment can be achieved when there is a strong meeting of minds.

10 WEDNESDAY

Moon Age Day 4   Moon Sign Capricorn

am . . . .

pm . . . .
Progress may not be easy in practical matters today and tomorrow. Even if nothing is going very wrong, with the Moon in your solar twelfth house this is not an ideal time to push yourself too hard. It pays to be aware of your environment and to take note of any changes that have occurred there.

11 THURSDAY

Moon Age Day 5   Moon Sign Capricorn

am . . . .

pm . . . .
Career incentives are well marked, though probably below the surface just for the moment. Today is about giving of your best, working quietly but confidently between now and the weekend. After all, that's the best way to create a favourable impression. Once you are away from work, be prepared to respond to some possible surprises.

12 FRIDAY   *Moon Age Day 6   Moon Sign Capricorn*

am . . . .

pm . . . .
Why not get together with friends today if it proves to be possible to do so? A somewhat quieter Aquarius than would usually be the case may still be in evidence, though by this evening trends change dramatically and a more up-front attitude is possible. There is much to be said for getting in touch with people around now.

13 SATURDAY   *Moon Age Day 7   Moon Sign Aquarius*

am . . . .

pm . . . .
The lunar high offers the best day of the month to break loose and do whatever takes your fancy. If your time is your own this weekend you can afford to spend it having fun in good company. As you move about you can do yourself a great deal of good by demonstrating your amazing capacity for successfully mixing business with pleasure.

14 SUNDAY   *Moon Age Day 8   Moon Sign Aquarius*

am . . . .

pm . . . .
A high degree of luck is available to you right now, and you can make gains by simply being in the right place and by following your intuition. Progress is possible in money matters, even if it is only a case of sorting things out in your own mind. Most important of all today is the way you make use of the opportunity to enjoy yourself.

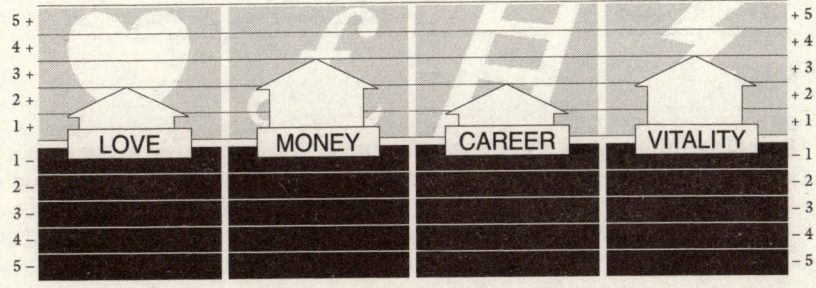

15 MONDAY
Moon Age Day 9   Moon Sign Pisces

am . . . .

pm . . . .
As far as relationships are concerned at this time, you can use love matches to expand your personal horizons and to learn more about life in general. Not that you need to restrict yourself in terms of the people you mix with. On the contrary, trends assist you to be very approachable and as interesting as Aquarius usually turns out to be.

16 TUESDAY
Moon Age Day 10   Moon Sign Pisces

am . . . .

pm . . . .
You should be able to continue to make more than satisfactory progress in your professional and business life, and you can also afford to be very ambitious. This is probably the most opportune part of the month for approaching those who are in positions of authority or influence. The idea is to persuade them to work on your behalf.

17 WEDNESDAY
Moon Age Day 11   Moon Sign Aries

am . . . .

pm . . . .
Life can be a constant learning process and this is certainly the case for the typical Aquarian subject. Don't assume today that you know everything about any topic. There are always going to be individuals around from whom you can learn something new, and the more you pay attention the greater will be your appreciation of life's nuances.

18 THURSDAY
Moon Age Day 12   Moon Sign Aries

am . . . .

pm . . . .
Being on the move is the order of the day. You have scope to get what you want by being positive and by getting others to follow your lead. Attitude is always important but especially so around now. People have a wide variety of views and it is your job to sort out the wheat from the chaff. Look for opportunities to play the matchmaker.

19 FRIDAY   *Moon Age Day 13   Moon Sign Aries*

am . . . .

pm . . . .
Family matters are accentuated today. You can benefit from the comforts
of home and also from activities that are taking place there. Trends
suggest that there are strong emotional ties in your thinking. All the
more reason to seek the advice of your partner or family members before
you take decisions.

20 SATURDAY   *Moon Age Day 14   Moon Sign Taurus*

am . . . .

pm . . . .
There is much to be said for venturing out into the wider world and
expanding your horizons as much as you can. Venus is now in a
favourable position for you when it comes to making important new
discoveries and friendships that have potential to last a lifetime. A day to
get out and about and enjoy the strong social impulses.

21 SUNDAY   *Moon Age Day 15   Moon Sign Taurus*

am . . . .

pm . . . .
Capitalise on career boosts that are available at any time now, though this
may not be easy on a Sunday. Nevertheless you can do yourself some
professional good by thinking through your strategy for next week. The
focus is also on sport under present trends, and you may decide it's time
to test yourself in some way.

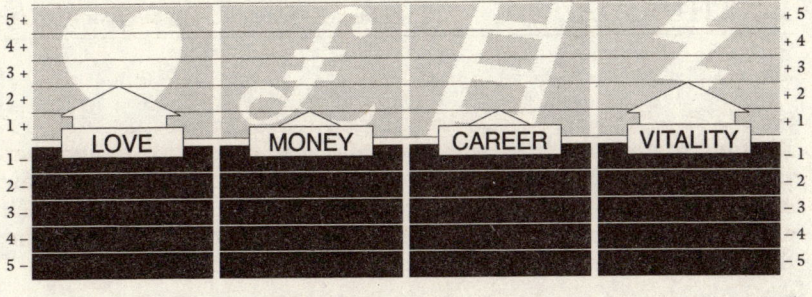

22 MONDAY
Moon Age Day 16   Moon Sign Gemini

am . . . .

pm . . . .
Romantic and social developments are well marked this week. Your best
approach is to stay involved as much as possible and avoid being left out
of any gossip that is taking place in your vicinity. Actually you can do
yourself more than a little good by listening to idle chatter, because
below the surface may be some excellent ideas.

23 TUESDAY
Moon Age Day 17   Moon Sign Gemini

am . . . .

pm . . . .
Be prepared to look towards higher purposes, though bear in mind that
at least some other people may not understand the complicated working
of your mind. Why not seek out individuals who are as unique and far-
sighted as you are? Confidence to do the right thing in a romantic sense
is clearly growing now.

24 WEDNESDAY
Moon Age Day 18   Moon Sign Gemini

am . . . .

pm . . . .
Watch out for minor pitfalls today and beware of wandering into
situations you know are going to be difficult to control. The impression
you need to give at the moment is one that makes you appear fully in
command of everything. This will not be helped if you are clearly out of
your depth or struggling to find answers that won't appear.

25 THURSDAY
Moon Age Day 19   Moon Sign Cancer

am . . . .

pm . . . .
It's time to discover the new or the unusual that exists all around you.
How exciting life can be, and how keen you should be to know
everything about it! You thrive best when you are educating yourself
about the world, and that is something you have a chance to do at this
time. New starts at work could be beneficial in the longer term.

26 FRIDAY

Moon Age Day 20   Moon Sign Cancer

am . . . .

pm . . . .
It pays to keep up the good work when it comes to supporting anyone who is having a hard time at the moment. Remember that in a social sense not everything you do has to have a purpose – except your enjoyment. If you bear this in mind you may also discover that when you stop looking for deliberate gains they come along anyway.

27 SATURDAY

Moon Age Day 21   Moon Sign Leo

am . . . .

pm . . . .
Any tiredness today can be partly blamed on the lunar low. This might not be the most dynamic weekend of the year, but you can ensure it is warm and comfortable, and it has much to recommend it in a personal sense. If you need to feel that people are on your side around now, the best sort of reassurance shouldn't be far away.

28 SUNDAY

Moon Age Day 22   Moon Sign Leo

am . . . .

pm . . . .
This might well be another day that lacks some of the sparkle you are seeking, though you can still enjoy yourself if you don't have too many expectations. Rules and regulations could easily get on your nerves, and despite the feelings of security on offer at home, you may even feel somewhat tied down there. A few excursions might help.

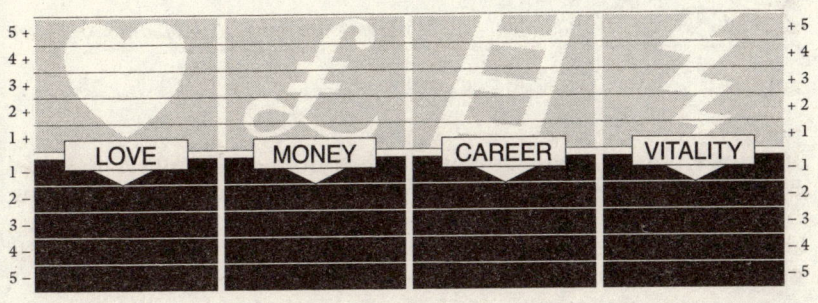

29 MONDAY
Moon Age Day 23   Moon Sign Virgo

am . . . .

pm . . . .
Around this time you may have a chance to show people you didn't know very well before just how engaging and charming you can be. The lunar low is out of the way so you can afford to be right up there pitching with the best of them. Don't get too tied up with the complications of the lives of other people – you have enough of your own!

30 TUESDAY
Moon Age Day 24   Moon Sign Virgo

am . . . .

pm . . . .
Contentious matters could now arise, and it might be difficult to get away from issues you would rather ignore altogether. In a personal sense it's possible for you to make a good impression on others, and you might also discover you have an admirer you didn't suspect. Whether that pleases you remains to be seen!

1 WEDNESDAY
Moon Age Day 25   Moon Sign Libra

am . . . .

pm . . . .
There is a strong social theme about as December gets started. If you demonstrate your characteristic affability, people should actively want to have you around, especially at social gatherings. Your ability to make things go with a swing is emphasised, as is your capacity to talk, even on subjects you know nothing about.

2 THURSDAY
Moon Age Day 26   Moon Sign Libra

am . . . .

pm . . . .
Independence and anything unusual are both issues for today. 'Routine' is not a word that suits Aquarius for the moment, and it's worth seeking out those who are as off-the-wall as you are capable of being. Keep up the good work when it comes to projecting your image to a wider audience, and don't be afraid to make yourself heard.

3 FRIDAY

Moon Age Day 27   Moon Sign Scorpio

am . . . .

pm . . . .
Being fond of your independence is fine, though you needn't try to go it
alone too much at the moment. There are ways and means of getting
others involved and you know them all. Aquarius needs constant support,
not because it is in any way inadequate but because things go better when
they are shared with someone else.

4 SATURDAY

Moon Age Day 28   Moon Sign Scorpio

am . . . .

pm . . . .
Be prepared to respond if you feel a friend or a social contact is very
opinionated around now. By all means put them in their place, though
you should do so as gently as possible. You know when you are correct
in your opinions, but there may be the odd time at the moment when
this is not entirely true.

5 SUNDAY

Moon Age Day 29   Moon Sign Sagittarius

am . . . .

pm . . . .
You should be in your element when you are visiting people. This is the
case at the best of times, but even more so under present planetary
trends. There are influences around now that encourage you to seek out
the weird and wonderful in life, to positive effect. Confidence remains
high and your social instincts are very finely tuned.

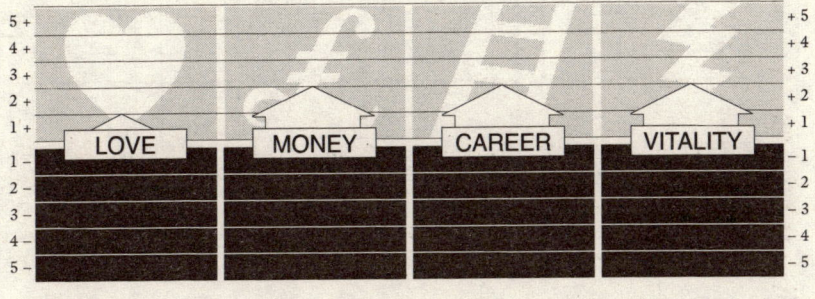

December 2010

YOUR MONTH AT A GLANCE

⊕ = Opportunities are around   ⊖ = Be on the defensive   ⬤ = Life is pretty ordinary

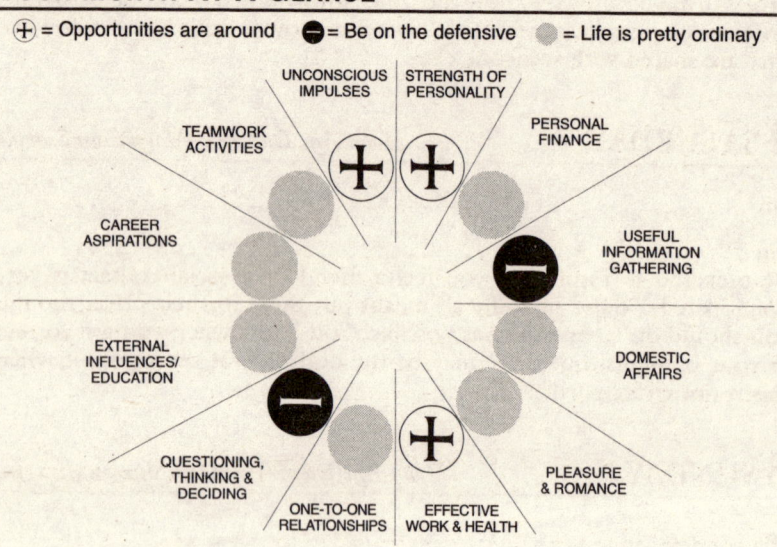

DECEMBER HIGHS AND LOWS

Here I show you how the rhythms of the Moon will affect you this month. Like the tide, your energies and abilities will rise and fall with its pattern. When it is above the centre line, go for it, when it is below, you should be resting.

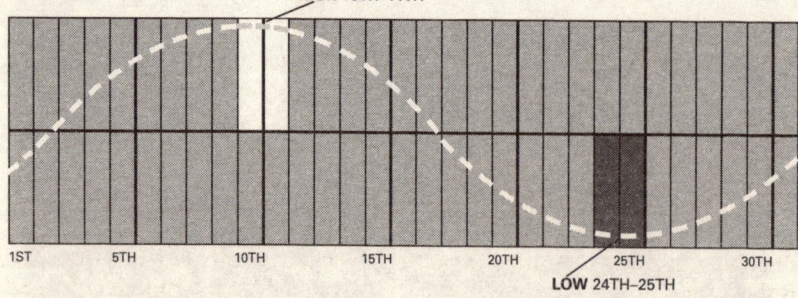

150

6 MONDAY
Moon Age Day 0   Moon Sign Sagittarius

am . . . .

pm . . . .
It pays to be a little careful today because your emotional suggestibility is to the fore. Right now you could believe exactly what you want to believe, and that can be something of a mistake. Even if most people appear to be kind, there might be the odd selfish individual, and that is the one you need to watch out for.

7 TUESDAY
Moon Age Day 1   Moon Sign Capricorn

am . . . .

pm . . . .
There are now positive highlights available in group activities and these could become more obvious as the week goes on. You can afford to put yourself at the centre of things, which suits you down to the ground though it might mean you are quite busy. Aquarius has scope to be very enterprising under present trends, and there are gains to be made.

8 WEDNESDAY
Moon Age Day 2   Moon Sign Capricorn

am . . . .

pm . . . .
Your chief ability in your career is your ability to establish contact with other people at an intense level. Communication is now the key to success. There isn't anything particularly unusual about this fact as far as you are concerned, but it is the depth of the ties you establish that might prove to be so important at this time.

9 THURSDAY
Moon Age Day 3   Moon Sign Capricorn

am . . . .

pm . . . .
A slightly quieter interlude is possible for the moment, and this is linked to the presence of the Moon in your solar twelfth house. This is a state of affairs that always comes just ahead of the lunar high, as if it is intended to be a time to plan your most progressive moves of the month. An ideal time to contact those who are at a distance.

10 FRIDAY

Moon Age Day 4   Moon Sign Aquarius

am . . . .

pm . . . .

The enthusiasm you invest in all matters now enables you to capitalise on the good fortune that is available. Even if this isn't anything major, it could be important to you and might pave the way to greater successes later on. The lunar high encourages you to spend time with loved ones and find ways to have fun that you have not tried before.

11 SATURDAY ☿

Moon Age Day 5   Moon Sign Aquarius

am . . . .

pm . . . .

Now you should be overflowing with ideas and more willing than ever to test your luck. Take advantage of whatever is going on around you in a social sense, and be ready to do all you can to make the most of new situations and positive meetings. Don't forget to show your concern for family members.

12 SUNDAY ☿

Moon Age Day 6   Moon Sign Pisces

am . . . .

pm . . . .

Trends support an impressionable interlude in which you could be easily influenced by others. There's nothing wrong with this just as long as you are aware that not everyone is as honest or decent as you are. With little Mercury now having passed into your solar twelfth house, there could be times today when you will be happy to withdraw.

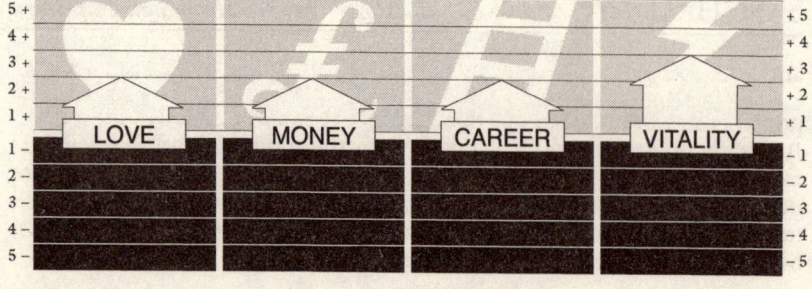

13 MONDAY ☿ *Moon Age Day 7   Moon Sign Pisces*

am . . . .

pm . . . .
In a professional sense you are best suited to situations in which you can make contact with any number of other people. This offers you the opportunity to use many of your ideas and to capitalise on the responses that these bring. Any unexpected assistance that is on offer today can make a great deal of difference in your life.

14 TUESDAY ☿ *Moon Age Day 8   Moon Sign Pisces*

am . . . .

pm . . . .
The focus is on a sense of restlessness at the moment. With the Moon where it is in your chart you could find it difficult to settle to anything specific, and might wish you were doing something else. Bear in mind that you would probably get tired of that too! All the same, doing two or more things at the same time should be easy right now.

15 WEDNESDAY ☿ *Moon Age Day 9   Moon Sign Aries*

am . . . .

pm . . . .
A far slower and more studied approach to plans and objectives seems to be in order around this time. Your best approach is to keep to one or two simple priorities and try not to crowd your schedule more than is necessary. Has it only now occurred to you properly that Christmas is imminent?

16 THURSDAY ☿ *Moon Age Day 10   Moon Sign Aries*

am . . . .

pm . . . .
In a social sense it looks as though trends continue to be very favourable. Groups of people provide the greatest stimulus at the moment and your general motto can be 'the more, the merrier'. Social gatherings are well marked, and you can use them to provide you with plenty of good ideas. Mixing and mingling should now be second nature.

17 FRIDAY ☿ *Moon Age Day 11 Moon Sign Taurus*

am . . . .

pm . . . .
Are your own drives and feelings slightly at odds with those of the people you are mixing with? This could bring the possibility of a disagreement you could quite easily do without at this time. It would be better under most circumstances today to withdraw from any issue that looks as though it might get out of control.

18 SATURDAY ☿ *Moon Age Day 12 Moon Sign Taurus*

am . . . .

pm . . . .
If emotions at home are now quite close to the surface, this is the right time to try and foster a new sense of togetherness amongst family members. You needn't try to do everything yourself, especially in the run-up to Christmas. It would be better by far to let someone else make some of the decisions you are trying to deal with alone.

19 SUNDAY ☿ *Moon Age Day 13 Moon Sign Taurus*

am . . . .

pm . . . .
The spotlight is on your eagerness to make a good impression and to get on well with just about everyone. That's fine, though it may not be possible under all circumstances. If some people seem determined to be awkward, you may have to disagree with them. This doesn't mean your popularity is going to disappear overnight.

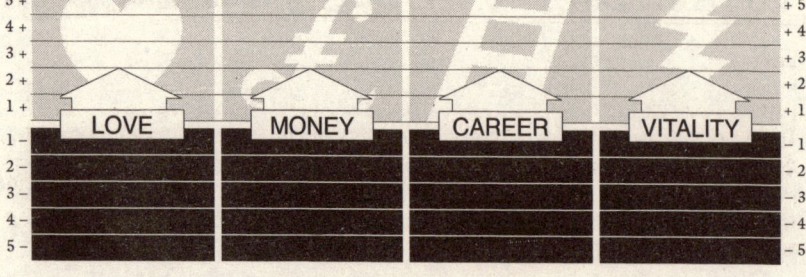

20 MONDAY ☿ *Moon Age Day 14   Moon Sign Gemini*

am . . . .

pm . . . .
Professional initiatives could be extremely important at the start of this particular week. At the same time it's worth keeping one eye on the needs of your family. You have what it takes to get most schemes to work out more or less as you planned, and positive progress is within your grasp, even if you have to change your mind. Financial gains are possible.

21 TUESDAY ☿ *Moon Age Day 15   Moon Sign Gemini*

am . . . .

pm . . . .
There is much to be said for focusing on your work at this time, and you probably won't take kindly to anyone trying to pull the professional rug from under you. Today is about ensuring that your ideas are creative and that you show good judgement in decisions you make now. Treat the secrets of your friends with great respect.

22 WEDNESDAY ☿ *Moon Age Day 16   Moon Sign Cancer*

am . . . .

pm . . . .
Although this is the start of the festive season, and therefore a potentially optimistic period as far as you are concerned, there is a slight risk that you will lose your sense of proportion in some situations. Try not to worry and certainly don't fantasise about what might go wrong. In the main you can ensure this is a successful day.

23 THURSDAY ☿ *Moon Age Day 17   Moon Sign Cancer*

am . . . .

pm . . . .
If you like people and enjoy social contact there is every chance that you will be at your very best for the Christmas period. You have what it takes to deal successfully with all sorts of people around now, and especially those who have special needs of one sort or another. This is a time during which it should be easy to count your own blessings.

24 FRIDAY ☿ *Moon Age Day 18   Moon Sign Leo*

am . . . .

pm . . . .
A very slight word of warning is that the lunar low coincides with
Christmas Eve and Christmas Day for you this year. Although you
needn't allow this to take the shine off your celebrations, it could make
you tire more easily than would normally be the case. It may also support
a slightly more nostalgic and emotional interlude than usual.

25 SATURDAY ☿ *Moon Age Day 19   Moon Sign Leo*

am . . . .

pm . . . .
Bear in mind that some of your plans for today might have to be altered
at the last minute, but the way to deal with the odd difficult situation is
to react by instinct, something you are very good at doing. Travelling
around may not be at the top of your agenda, and there are good reasons
to opt for a stay-at-home Christmas if that is possible.

26 SUNDAY ☿ *Moon Age Day 20   Moon Sign Virgo*

am . . . .

pm . . . .
The lunar low is now out of the way, offering you scope to make the
period between now and the New Year one of movement and merriment.
You will be settling to what is expected of you during the Christmas
break and making the most of the social trends that are so favourable.
You may even be able to make the odd financial gain today.

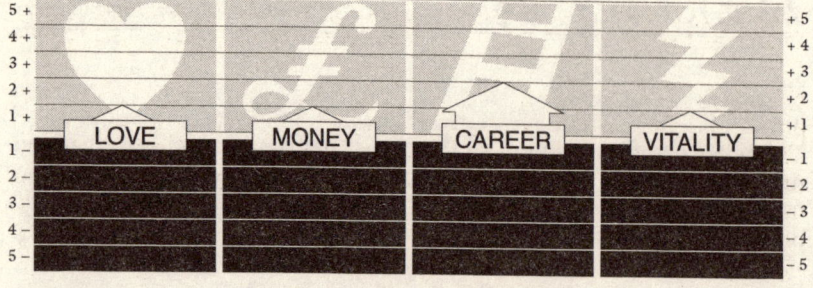

27 MONDAY ☿ *Moon Age Day 21 Moon Sign Virgo*

am . . . .

pm
You need to find the space and the opportunity to retire from the stresses and strains of everyday life – not that these ever bother you too much. Even if you are given the chance to take a break, you may not choose to do so. Look to new group activities later.

28 TUESDAY ☿ *Moon Age Day 22 Moon Sign Libra*

am . . . .

pm . . . .
There are some possible unrealistic fantasies to deal with today, possibly from the direction of your friends or perhaps family members. On the plus side, the romantic trends look especially intriguing and potentially rewarding now.

29 WEDNESDAY ☿ *Moon Age Day 23 Moon Sign Libra*

am . . . .

pm . . . .
Personal liberty could be the main issue at this time, and you need to capitalise on opportunities to do your own thing. Don't be talked out of following your own convictions, and be prepared to go an extra mile to really get what you want.

30 THURSDAY ☿ *Moon Age Day 24 Moon Sign Scorpio*

am . . . .

pm . . . .
True to your Aquarian nature, you function best at the moment when you are involved in a team or some sort of social group. Whether you are working or simply finding ways to have fun, you can make sure this is an eventful and generally rewarding day.

31 FRIDAY *Moon Age Day 25 Moon Sign Scorpio*

am . . . .

pm . . . .
This is not a time to expect too much if you push yourself forward all the time. Rewards are more likely to come from genuine co-operation and from taking your place amongst others. Once again the romantic possibilities look extremely good.

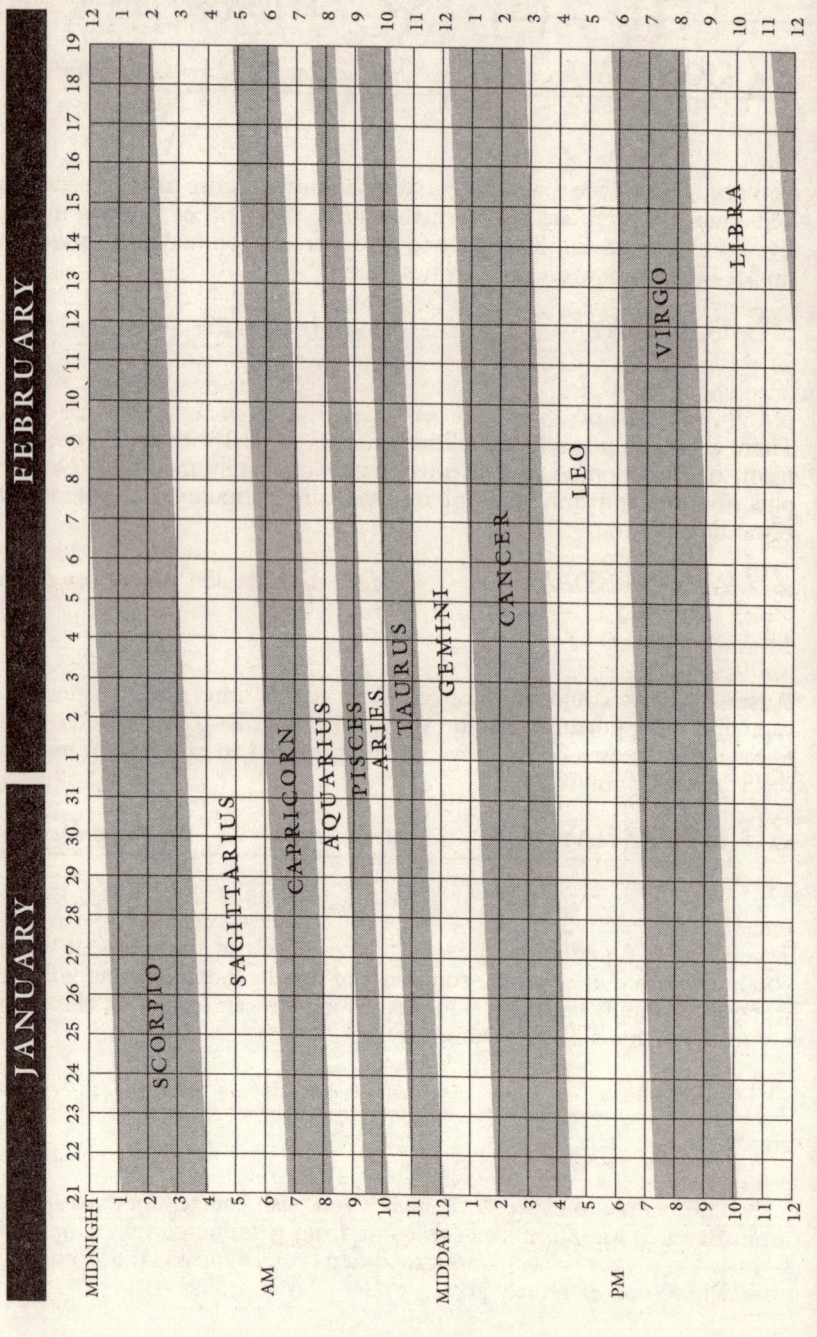

JANUARY   FEBRUARY

21 22 23 24 25 26 27 28 29 30 31 1 2 3 4 5 6 7 8 9 10 11 12 13 14 15 16 17 18 19

MIDNIGHT 12 1 2 3 4 5 6 7 8 9 10 11 12 1 2 3 4 5 6 7 8 9 10 11 12

AM

MIDDAY 12

PM

SCORPIO

SAGITTARIUS

CAPRICORN

AQUARIUS

PISCES

ARIES

TAURUS

GEMINI

CANCER

LEO

VIRGO

LIBRA

158

THE ZODIAC, PLANETS AND CORRESPONDENCES

The Earth revolves around the Sun once every calendar year, so when viewed from Earth the Sun appears in a different part of the sky as the year progresses. In astrology, these parts of the sky are divided into the signs of the zodiac and this means that the signs are organised in a circle. The circle begins with Aries and ends with Pisces.

Taking the zodiac sign as a starting point, astrologers then work with all the positions of planets, stars and many other factors to calculate horoscopes and birth charts and tell us what the stars have in store for us.

The table below shows the planets and Elements for each of the signs of the zodiac. Each sign belongs to one of the four Elements: Fire, Air, Earth or Water. Fire signs are creative and enthusiastic; Air signs are mentally active and thoughtful; Earth signs are constructive and practical; Water signs are emotional and have strong feelings.

It also shows the metals and gemstones associated with, or corresponding with, each sign. The correspondence is made when a metal or stone possesses properties that are held in common with a particular sign of the zodiac.

Finally, the table shows the opposite of each star sign – this is the opposite sign in the astrological circle.

Placed	Sign	Symbol	Element	Planet	Metal	Stone	Opposite
1	Aries	Ram	Fire	Mars	Iron	Bloodstone	Libra
2	Taurus	Bull	Earth	Venus	Copper	Sapphire	Scorpio
3	Gemini	Twins	Air	Mercury	Mercury	Tiger's Eye	Sagittarius
4	Cancer	Crab	Water	Moon	Silver	Pearl	Capricorn
5	Leo	Lion	Fire	Sun	Gold	Ruby	Aquarius
6	Virgo	Maiden	Earth	Mercury	Mercury	Sardonyx	Pisces
7	Libra	Scales	Air	Venus	Copper	Sapphire	Aries
8	Scorpio	Scorpion	Water	Pluto	Plutonium	Jasper	Taurus
9	Sagittarius	Archer	Fire	Jupiter	Tin	Topaz	Gemini
10	Capricorn	Goat	Earth	Saturn	Lead	Black Onyx	Cancer
11	Aquarius	Waterbearer	Air	Uranus	Uranium	Amethyst	Leo
12	Pisces	Fishes	Water	Neptune	Tin	Moonstone	Virgo

Foulsham books can be found in all
good bookshops or direct from
www.foulsham.com